Rocky Mountain Tour

Estes Park – Rocky Mountain National Park – Grand Lake

Suzanne Silverthorn

Illustrated with 300 Historical Postcards, Photographs & Ephemera

ONE OF THE MANY CHARMINGLY BEAUTIFUL LITTLE MOUNTAIN LAKES
ROCKY MOUNTAIN NATIONAL - ESTES PARK, COLORADO
A NATURAL, WILD, BEAUTIFUL AND PEACEFUL IMMENSITY OF HEALTHFUL OUTDOORS
Burlington Route - Direct to the Park

FALL RIVER ROAD ACROSS THE CONTINENTAL DIVIDE,
ROCKY MOUNTAIN NATIONAL (ESTES) PARK.
REACHED VIA UNION PACIFIC SYSTEM.

Schiffer Publishing Ltd

4880 Lower Valley Road, Atglen, PA 19310

Disclaimer

Copyright © 2008 by Suzanne Silverthorn
Library of Congress Control Number: 2007942549

Designed by RoS
Type set in Humansta521 BT

ISBN: 978-0-7643-2848-0
Printed in China

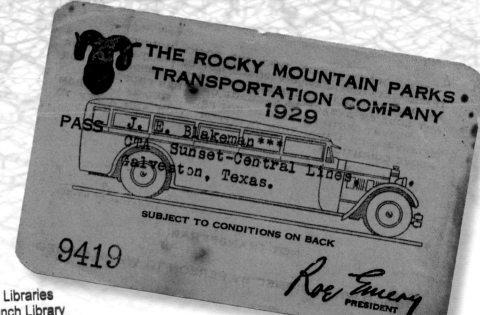

Dedication

This book is dedicated to the owners, past and present, of the rustic lodges that have welcomed thousands of guests during their visits to Rocky Mountain National Park and the nearby towns of Estes Park and Grand Lake over the past one hundred years.

FERN LAKE.   ROCKY MOUNTAIN NATIONAL PARK.

Contents

Acknowledgments

Many people have helped make this book possible. The author expresses appreciation to those who answered questions, helped with research, and shared collectibles to assist with this project. Special thanks to Sybil Barnes, reference librarian for the Estes Park Library and Library Tech for Rocky Mountain National Park, for her invaluable assistance and support. Thanks also to Bob Scott and Jane Kemp of Grand Lake, and David Scarbrough, owner of Mountain Time in Estes Park, who gave the author permission to photograph items from their collections, as well as Mac Ruske, who shared his knowledge of the Grand Lake area.

Others who assisted include Mr. and Mrs. Fred Bell, Lake Haven; Becky and Steve Childs, Glen Haven General Store; William Jones, River Forks Inn; Becky Latanich, Estes Park Museum and Estes Park Library; Bill and Juanita Martin, Allenspark Lodge Bed and Breakfast; Jenna MacGregor, Historic Park Theatre; Lulie and Jack Melton, YMCA of the Rockies/Lula W. Dorsey Museum; Elizabeth M. Mills Kiley and Eryn Mills Kiley, Enos Mills Cabin; Steve Mitchell, Estes Park Library; Greg Raile, Stonebridge Technology Services; Rex Roth, former owner of Wild Basin Lodge; Lois H. Smith, Baldpate Inn; Jerry and Carol Zahourek, Elkhorn Lodge; and Bill and Marta Zick of Grand Lake. Thanks also to the Stanley Museum, Kingfield, Maine; the Stanley Museum of Colorado, Estes Park; the Colorado Historical Society in Denver; and the Grand Lake Area Historical Society for loaning images from their archives.

Lastly, the author extends thanks to her family, especially fellow author and mother Dian Zillner, for her research and ongoing encouragement, as well as husband Mark and son Prather who stayed behind during numerous research trips.

Additional recognition is extended to Schiffer Publishing Ltd. and its excellent staff.

Introduction

Near a mountain range north and west of Denver, Colorado, the land was originally homesteaded for farming and ranching, but the settlers soon discovered that providing room and board to visiting hunters and adventurers was a more profitable way to make a living. The sender of a postcard picturing a scenic landscape and mailed more than one hundred years ago reflected the sentiments of many of those early day visitors, "Isn't this beautiful? I cannot imagine a more delightful place. My two weeks have been perfect."

By 1915 when Rocky Mountain National Park was dedicated as the nation's tenth national park, the towns bordering the new attraction, Estes Park on the east and Grand Lake on the west, were eager to capitalize on the attention by expanding existing guest lodges and constructing new ones. With the mobility of travelers on the rise due to the popularity of the railroad, an entrepreneurial businessman named Roe Emery recognized an even greater opportunity to promote the region with his creation of "The Circle Tour," a scenic multi-day bus excursion through Rocky Mountain National Park. Emery eventually became known as the "father" of modern tourism in Colorado and his legacy includes thousands of postcards that were sent by Circle Tour travelers describing their adventures to friends and family back home. Examples of those experiences are presented throughout this book.

The Circle Tour excursions began shortly after the completion of Fall River Road in 1920, which linked Estes Park and Grand Lake along the breathtaking drive through Rocky Mountain National Park. Tourists boarded one of Emery's twelve-passenger buses from the railroad station in Denver, where they traveled through scenic Big Thompson Canyon and on to Estes Park. From there, guests could continue through Rocky Mountain National Park to Grand Lake before the travelers returned to Denver. Circle Tour packages could last from two to six days, affording guests a variety of options to enjoy a multitude of sights along the way. Today, visitors continue to enjoy many of these same delights and can stay in some of the original lodges as they experience their own "circle tour," with ample opportunities to send a postcard or two.

Early postcards from Emery's Circle Tour era are popular with today's collectors. They picture the historic lodges, lakes, and scenery from the period. The most sought after postcards can cost as much as $60 each. Many collectors specialize in postcards picturing images produced by William T. "Billy" Parke, or Fred Payne Clatworthy, both of whom made their home in Estes Park in the early twentieth century. Later postcards dating from the 1920s to the 1950s, mostly produced in black and white by Harold Sanborn of the Sanborn Souvenir Co., Denver, are also in demand. Together, the postcards illustrate the surrounding beauty of the area and help tell the story of Colorado tourism over the past one hundred years.

Part One:

The Circle Tour

The Circle Tour was created following Roe Emery's successful enterprise at Glacier National Park in Montana, where his tour buses complemented train excursions provided by the Great Northern Railroad. In 1913 the Burlington Railroad saw similar promise in the mountains near Estes Park and convinced Emery to bring his tourist travel business to Colorado. In 1916 Emery purchased F. O. Stanley's Estes Park Transportation Company and created the Rocky Mountain Parks Transportation Company, replacing Stanley's famous steamers with gas-operated automobiles.

Three years later and after much controversy, Emery obtained a transportation monopoly from the National Park Service to transport visitors into Rocky Mountain National Park. When Fall River Road was opened in 1920, it connected Estes Park with Grand Lake, giving Emery an opportunity to develop his 240-mile scenic tour that began and ended in Denver with overnight stops in Estes Park, Grand Lake, and Idaho Springs, while crossing the Continental Divide twice. Emery worked with the railroads to promote the trip, which could be included in railroad fares from other parts of the country. Emery sold his transportation company in 1952 while Colorado was enjoying its success as one of the most popular tourism destinations in the United States. He died the next year at the age of seventy-eight.

Studio portrait of Roe Emery, circa late 1920s – early 1930s. At the time he was president of his Rocky Mountain Parks Transportation Company. *Courtesy of the Colorado Historical Society.*

Postcard folders from the Rocky Mountain National Park Circle Tour. The one on the left is from the Sanborn Souvenir Co., Denver, circa 1930s. The other is from H. H. Tammen Co. from the 1920s. Roe Emery of the Denver-based Rocky Mountain Parks Transportation Company originated the Circle Tour circa 1922. $8-10 each.

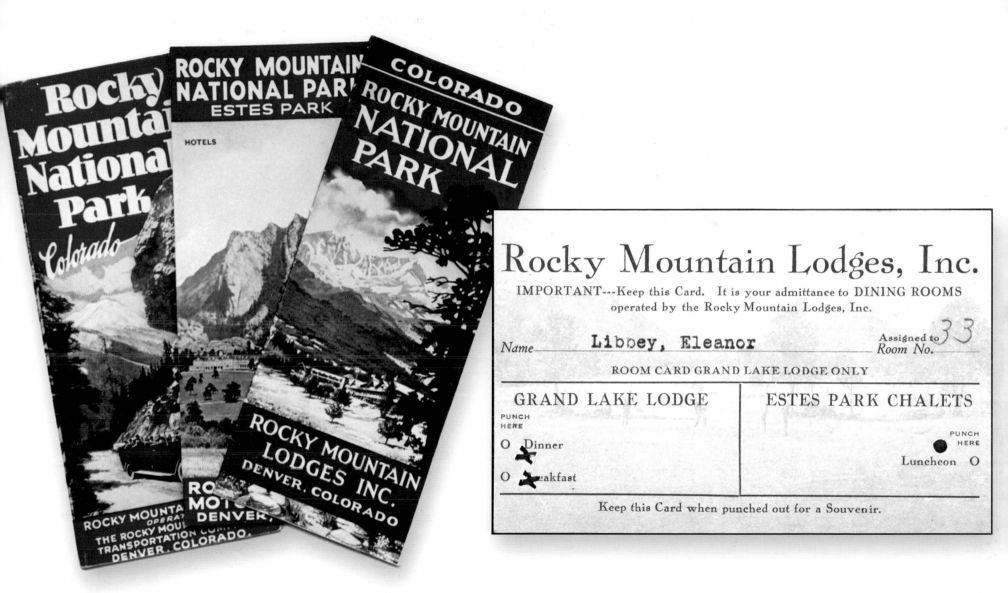

Brochures from different eras promoting the trips and hotels featured on Emery's Circle Tour. The trips could last two to six days according to tourists' wishes. On the two-day tour, travelers left Denver at 8 a.m. and arrived at Estes Park for lunch at noon, left Estes at 2:30 p.m., and arrived at Grand Lake at 6 p.m. for an overnight stay. At 8:30 the next morning, the bus left Grand Lake, stopped at Idaho Springs, and arrived in Denver at 4:30 p.m. The Placer Inn in Idaho Springs was the stopping point for lunch on the second day. It was used for several years as a lunch stop both before and after Emery's association with the Hot Springs Hotel. The red brochure is from the early 1920s, the middle brochure was issued before 1929, and the newest brochure dates from 1936-37. $15-20 each.

Rocky Mountain Lodges, Inc. was the lodging division of the company developed by Roe Emery to make his tour business complete. His Rocky Mountain Parks Transportation Co. negotiated with Rocky Mountain Lodges, Inc., controlled by A. D. Lewis of Estes Park, to purchase the Lewiston Chalets and Grand Lake Lodge, according to a report in the *Estes Park Trail* on January 5, 1923. He paid $75,000 for the transaction, and then renamed the Lewiston Chalets the Estes Park Chalets. Shown is a meal ticket issued to a passenger from the Circle Tour, providing the guest with lunch at the Estes Park Chalets and dinner and breakfast at Grand Lake Lodge. The ticket was also used as a room card at Grand Lake Lodge. Circa 1920s, $20+.

5999. New Union Station, Denver, Colorado

Many of the Circle Tour passengers arrived by rail and began their journey from Union Station in Denver. The price of the Circle Tour could be included in their rail ticket as part of an overall "See America First" summer excursion package promoted by the national parks and the railroads. The cost for transportation and hotel accommodations was $33 for a two-day trip, $39 for a three-day trip, $45 for a four-day trip, and $60 for the six-day trip. The six-day trip included two nights at Estes Park Chalets, a side trip to Bear Lake, two nights at Grand Lake Lodge with boating, fishing, and hiking, and one night at the Hot Springs Hotel in Idaho Springs. HHT Co. postcard of Union Station, circa mid 1920s, $3-5.

ESTES PARK CHALETS · GRAND LAKE LODGE · HOT SPRINGS HOTEL · ROCKY MOUNTAIN NATIONAL PARK ·

This souvenir decal was available to guests on the Circle Tour listing the trip's major destinations. This image was also used on a 1924 company brochure describing the popularity of the area — 218,000 people had visited Rocky Mountain National Park the prior year with projections of 300,000 visitors for 1924. $35+.

426—Entering Thompson Cañon, Colorado on the New Highway from Loveland to Estes Park

Rocky Mountain National Park

409 Rapids Hill, Big Thompson Cañon, Colorado

Rocky Mountain National Park

A new highway was constructed in 1937. This Sanborn Souvenir postcard shows the entrance to Big Thompson Canyon and the new roadway. $3-5.

One of the most scenic sights along the Circle Tour came soon after leaving Denver, when passengers entered Big Thompson Canyon. The first road to connect Loveland and Estes Park along Big Thompson River was built in 1904. Shown is the road as it was being used in the canyon in the 1920s. The hand-colored postcard was published by F. P. Clatworthy, of Estes Park. $15+.

The rapids in Big Thompson Canyon in the late 1930s. The trip through the canyon on U.S. Highway 34 still includes the beautiful scenery that has attracted sightseers for more than a century. Sanborn Souvenir Co., Denver. $3-5.

Author's family postcard dated July 21, 1962 showing Big Thompson Canyon and its sheer rock wall formations. Big Thompson River starts near Estes Park in the Rocky Mountains and flows east through the canyon. At the end of the canyon, the river exits into a flat area west of Loveland. This Sanborn postcard shows the canyon much as it looked on the evening of July 31, 1976 — before a thunderstorm dumped nearly a foot of rain into the canyon. The ensuing flash flood turned the canyon into a wall of water reaching nineteen feet high. Everything in its path was destroyed, including the highway, cars, trucks, campers, homes, and businesses. The only way to safety was to climb the canyon walls. The death toll was estimated at 145. $3-5.

An observation team remained at the Dam Store at the mouth of Big Thompson Canyon near Loveland throughout the night of the 1976 flood. Rescue and evacuation teams left there at daylight to begin their heart-wrenching recovery work. R. R. Dietrich built the Dam Store in 1933. Additions have been made to the original structure as shown in this Sanborn postcard. It continues in business today. $3-5.

The Circle Tour arrived in Estes Park around lunchtime, with the first stop at the Estes Park Chalets. The lodge is located at the eastern entrance to Rocky Mountain National Park and overlooks Marys Lake. This hand-colored Clatworthy postcard shows the chalets and Emery's twelve passenger autos from the White Motor Company embarking on the next leg of the Circle Tour. $8-10.

The original Lewiston Chalets were built in 1919 by A. D. Lewis, who constructed part of the chalets around the remains of an earlier lodge built in 1913. In 1923 the property was sold to Roe Emery and his Rocky Mountain Parks Transportation Co. and the name was changed to Estes Park Chalets. Emery planned to use the chalets as housing for guests participating in his Circle Tour. On June 15, 1923, an advertisement in the *Estes Park Trail* described a house-warming party and dance to be held on June 22 to show off the renovations and additions Emery had made to the chalets. The dining room would seat 160 while the hotel could now accommodate 270 guests in fifty-seven rooms. The hotel also had a ballroom for dancing and a large lobby that was used for entertainment. HHT Co. postcard, $10+.

15377. Lewiston Chalets and Twins, Estes Park, Colorado
Rocky Mountain National Park

The lobby of the Estes Park Chalets as it looked when furnished with hickory furniture. Hand-colored postcard by F. P. Clatworthy, circa 1920s, $30+.

The dining room of the Estes Park Chalets as it appeared circa late 1930s or early 1940s. The furniture included hickory chairs like those used in the Grand Lake Lodge dining room during the same period. Sanborn postcard. $20+

A view of Marys Lake from the porch of the Estes Park Chalets. After a long ownership by Emery and later, the James family, the property was sold in 1969. After several owners, a fire in 1978, and financial hardships, the lodge, now called Marys Lake Lodge, has been totally restored and includes sixteen units plus forty condominiums. Flatiron Post Card Co., of Boulder, Colorado. $6-8.

After passengers enjoyed the hospitality of the Estes Park Chalets, they entered Rocky Mountain National Park and began their drive on Fall River Road. This narrow road was finished in 1920 and connected Estes Park and Grand Lake for the first time. This HHT Co. view shows Rocky Mountain Motor Co. touring cars crossing the new road in June with snowbanks nearly twenty-five feet high. $10+.

15760. June 25th—Fall River Road. Rocky Mountain National Park

A favorite stop on Fall River Road for any visitor was the Continental Divide, where river waters on the left in this picture flow to the Atlantic and the ones on the right, to the Pacific. H. H. Tammen Co. postcard, $8-10.

15647. Water to the Atlantic—Water to the Pacific. Milner Pass, Fall River Road

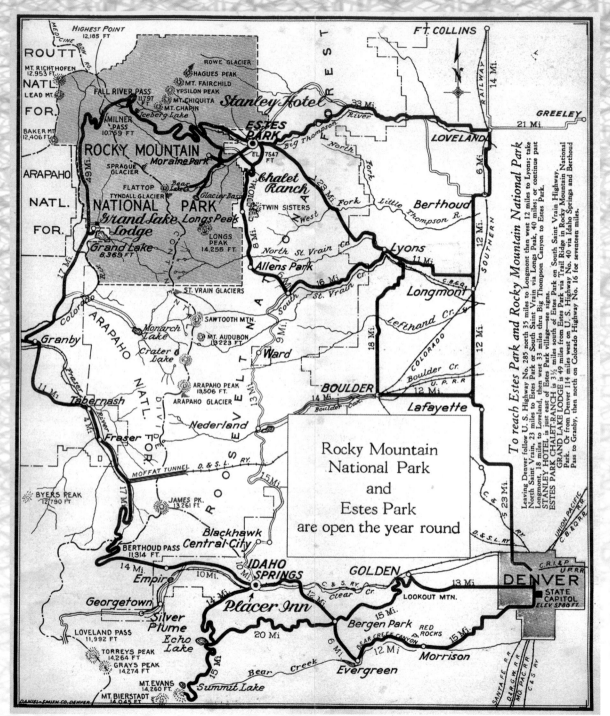

The map is titled "Rocky Mountain National Park and Estes Park are open the year round"

By 1932 the new Trail Ridge Road opened in Rocky Mountain National Park, allowing tourists to cross more quickly, and more safely, between Estes Park and Grand Lake. This road replaced Fall River Road on the tour route. The Rocky Mountain Motor Co. included this map in its brochure circa 1936-37. The names of hotels then owned or used by Emery to serve his Circle Tour guests are shown in large letters.

This view shows a Circle Tour bus making its way across Trail Ridge Road with a load of passengers in early summer. For tourists from warm climates, a chance to play in the snow was fun for all ages any time a trip was made across Trail Ridge. Postcard by Sanborn Souvenir Co., circa late 1930s to early 1940s, $3-5.

Several of the red Rocky Mountain Motor Co. tour buses are shown in this late 1930s to early 1940s view. These buses are hauling tourists on the western side of Trail Ridge Road. Sanborn Souvenir Co. postcard, $3-5.

A special treat for Trail Ridge Road tourists was a stop at the top of Fall River Pass, elevation 11,797 feet, to see the museum and visit the store, which was another of Roe Emery's enterprises when it opened for the start of the 1937 park season. The store has been in operation for over seventy years under various ownerships. This Sanborn postcard shows the popular landmark, which was named to the National Register of Historic Places in 1987. Circa 1930s to 1940s, $3-5.

BOATING ON GRAND LAKE, COLORADO
The "Rocky Mountain Limited" affords Excellent Service to Denver,
Connecting with Rocky Mountain Parks Transportation Company for Grand Lake

After Circle Tour passengers completed their trip over Fall River Pass in the early years, or Trail Ridge Road in the later years, they arrived in the Village of Grand Lake, the western entrance to Rocky Mountain National Park, and spent the night. The tour vehicles likely drove passengers by the lake to give them a look at the beautiful setting, as shown in this postcard by E. C. Kropp Co., of Milwaukee, which also advertised the Rock Island Railroad as the "Route of the Rockies connecting with the Rocky Mountain Transportation Co. for service to Grand Lake." $6-8.

15711. Grand Lake and Rabbit Ear Range, Colorado. Rocky Mountain National Park

A view of Grand Lake showing Rabbit Ear Range in the background. A walkway and moored sailboat are also shown. The message on the back appears to have been written by a Circle Tour passenger: "We are bound for this spot for our overnight stay. Just having the time of my life. We are so nicely located. Oh! This bracing air and the beauty to behold – all under such perfect conditions." Circle Tour participants could choose to stay in Grand Lake either overnight or for several days. HHT Co. postcard, $6-8.

While in Grand Lake, the overnight stop for the Circle Tour was at Grand Lake Lodge, which Emery purchased in 1923. The lodge was built several years earlier on Rocky Mountain National Park property, with the park's permission, by A. D. Lewis, a hotelier from Estes Park. The lodge opened in the summer of 1920, just a few months before Fall River Road, which would link Estes Park and Grand Lake from June to September each year. The building in this Grand Lake Lodge view housed the lobby, dining room, kitchen, and other practical facilities. A Clatworthy hand-colored postcard, circa 1920s, $15+.

One-and two-room guest cabins were built behind and up a small hill from the Grand Lake Lodge's main building. An item in the *Estes Park Trail* in 1922 mentioned that A. D. Lewis was making improvements to the lodge: ten new cabins were being built and a new dormitory, which included a recreation hall. A 110-volt electric plant had also been added and some remodeling was done to the interior of the main building. Twenty additional cottages were to be built in 1923. A Clatworthy hand-colored postcard showing one of the cottages, $15+.

The most unique feature of the Grand Lake Lodge is a veranda, furnished with a variety of chairs and swings, and offering the best views in all of Grand Lake. The message on the back of this late 1920s postcard says, "They have some Indian dolls here you would love. Lots of Wild West things for sale. We will hear a lecture on birds and wildlife of the mountains and then go back to the cabin to bed." The lodge housed a gift shop for tourists that included Indian-made jewelry and rugs. A Clatworthy hand-colored postcard, $15+.

Shown is luggage decal labeled "Grand Lake Lodge, Rocky Mountain National Park." Circa late 1930s, $20+.

In 1926 Grand Lake Lodge had a capacity for 250 guests who paid from $42 to $49 a week for food and accommodations. This hand-colored Clatworthy postcard, mailed in 1929, shows the fireplace in the lobby that was particularly popular with guests. $15+.

A group picture of the employees at Grand Lake Lodge, circa 1940. The head of the Rocky Mountain Transportation Co., Roe Emery, is in the back row, second from right. The photograph shows the large number of people who were employed each summer at each lodge to make the Circle Tours the success they were year after year. Guests were entertained with activities in the evenings that included bingo, programs by a park naturalist, and sing-alongs, skits, and musicals presented by the staff. Employees even stood on the front porch to greet the guests as they arrived on the tour buses and sang, "Welcome, welcome to the Grand Lake Lodge. Welcome, welcome to the scenic view." *Courtesy of Bob Scott.*

This view shows one of the tour buses from Emery's Rocky Mountain Motor Co. parked in front of the lodge, perhaps waiting for 8:30 a.m. when the Circle Tour would begin its last leg of the two-day trip. Sanborn postcard, circa early 1940s, $10+.

Brothers Ted and I. B. James purchased Grand Lake Lodge and Emery's transportation company in 1953. Ted managed the lodge, while I. B. ran the transportation enterprise. This view shows the dining room with its original Old Hickory furniture. In the early 1960s, the lodge was in danger of being acquired by the Park Service, so the James brothers bought other private land to exchange for the parklands surrounding the lodge. In 1963 the swap was approved and the park boundaries were changed to exclude the lodge. Flatiron postcard, $8.

Fire struck the Grand Lake Lodge on July 19, 1973 after an explosion in the kitchen. When the fire trucks ran out of water, responders turned to the swimming pool and water was siphoned from the pool to extinguish the blaze. Significant damage was done to the structure and its contents and the lodge was closed for refurbishing until 1981. It was added to the National Register of Historic Places in 1993. Management of the lodge continued under four generations of the James family and longtime employee Bob Scott who joined the business in 1969. Flatiron postcard, $6-8. *Fire photo courtesy of Bob Scott.*

After the tourists returned to their seats in their tour bus or "auto stage" as it was called earlier, they resumed their journey on the return trip to Denver. After passing through Granby and Fraser, they began another mountain drive over Berthoud Pass. This early 1920s view shows the wonderful scenery as they traveled up 11,330 feet over the pass. An H. H. Tammen Co. postcard, $8-10.

15648. Berthoud Pass and Crater, Mt. Colorado

15706. Looking East from Berthoud Pass, Colorado

This Berthoud Pass view also dates from the 1920s. The pass was named after E. L. Berthoud, who had surveyed a wagon road from Golden, Colorado, to Salt Lake City in 1861. It included crossing the Continental Divide on what is now U.S. Highway 40. Berthoud was also one of the founders of the School of Mines at Golden. An H. H. Tammen Co. postcard, $8-10.

The last stop on most of the Circle Tours was Idaho Springs, forty miles west of Denver, where Emery sub-leased the Hot Springs Hotel from Joe Meyers so he could provide accommodations for his guests. Shown is the hotel, which was built in 1915. In addition to the hotel, there was also an annex and twenty-four cottages. When Emery used it for his tours circa 1924-1928, it had a capacity for 130 guests. $10-15.

The Hot Springs Hotel was part of a resort that included hot mineral baths as well as the pictured Natatorium, constructed in 1918, that housed a swimming pool. The "plunge bath" measured eighty-feet long, forty-feet wide, and three-to seven-feet deep. It had a springboard, rings, and a trapeze and was fed with warm mineral spring water. Unmarked postcard, $8-10.

The finest in the mountains, 34 miles west of Denver on U. S. 6 and U. S. 40 Highways. Banquet and party capacity to 500. Fine food. Rooms, Cocktail Lounge, Dancing. Special reservation telephone 106, Idaho Springs, Colorado, or Denver KEystone 0085

Headquarters for Skiers - Hunters - Fishermen - Tourists - Mountain Climbers

From 1924 to 1928 Circle Tour guests ate at least one meal in the dining room at the Hot Springs Hotel. Emery spent a good deal of money to enlarge the dining room so it could accommodate his guests. Before 1924 and after 1928, Circle Tour guests were accommodated by Placer Inn, a smaller establishment on Miner Street in downtown Idaho Springs. $10+.

In 1929 Roe Emery made another change to his business when he purchased the Stanley Hotel from its original owner, Freelan Oscar Stanley. He used it as a more expensive alternative for Circle Tour guests in Estes Park. The information on the back of this card reads, "The Stanley Hotels, affording the most pretentious accommodations in the National Park…offers all the delights of 'roughing it' in the mountains with all the comforts of Home." Also shown is a Circle Tour ticket dated July 23, 1930. It was for the two-day all expense tour that included transportation, meals, and lodging. Sanborn postcard, $6-8; Circle Tour ticket, $10+.

Shown are Rocky Mountain National Park souvenir playing cards produced by Rocky Mountain Motor Co. during the 1920s. The cards show different scenes encountered by Circle Tour travelers, and the various facilities in use, including the Stanley Hotel, Estes Park Chalets, Grand Lake Lodge, and Placer Inn. $50+.

This luggage label was issued by Rocky Mountain Motor Co. to include the Stanley Hotel as one of its properties. Circa early 1930s, $50+.

Song sheet circa 1930s to early 1940s used by the Rocky Mountain Motor Co. at its lodges during the Circle Tour. Shown is one of the company brochures featuring the newly acquired Stanley Hotel and an F. P. Clatworthy hand-colored postcard of the Estes Park Chalets. The other two stops are also represented on the song sheet; Grand Lake Lodge, accompanied by a Sanborn postcard, and Placer Inn, shown in a black and white Sanborn postcard. The songs sung by guests and staff included old favorites such as "My Wild Irish Rose," "In the Evening by the Moon Light," and "On Wisconsin." Postcards, $5-12. *Song sheet courtesy of Bob Scott.*

This later Rocky Mountain Motor Co. brochure is dated 1950 with its familiar red bus pictured on the front. Still popular, Emery's Circle Tour left Denver Union Rail Terminal each day from June 1 to September 15 and returned the following afternoon. The bus continued to stop for lunch at Estes Park and tour members spent the night in Grand Lake. Bus fare was $16 round trip. In a 1949 interview with the *Rocky Mountain News*, Emery, who by then was known as the "father" of Colorado's modern tourism industry, downplayed his notoriety, noting, "Colorado has the most beautiful and most bountiful scenic grandeur of the country. All I did was give people a chance to look at it." In 1952 Emery sold his transportation company to Gene Holmes and T. J. Manning. They, in turn, sold the business to brothers Ted and I. B. James in 1953. While bus tours continued from Denver to the Rocky Mountains, the transportation monopoly with the Park Service soon came to an end after more than thirty years. $10+.

530-ESTES PARK, COLORADO.

Part Two:

Estes Park

In addition to its popular two-and three-day trips through Estes Park, Rocky Mountain National Park, and Grand Lake, the Circle Tour offered travelers the option of remaining at each stop for longer periods with arrangements to rejoin the tour at a later time. Favorite outings during extended stopovers in Estes Park included traversing the various trails by foot or horseback, climbing Longs Peak, visiting the Stanley Hotel, or learning about the colorful history of the area.

W.T. PARKE, ESTES PARK, COLO.

LONG'S PEAK AND RANGE.

ESTES PARK COLORADO.

Isn't this beautiful? I cannot imagine a more delightful place. My two weeks has been perfect. Tomorrow morning leave for Denver. K. 8/6/05-

The land around Estes Park was originally used for farming and ranching, but settlers soon discovered that providing room and board to visiting hunters and adventurers was a more profitable way to make a living. An HHT Co. postcard shows the town of Estes Park as it grew to accommodate its new tourist industry. The bottom postcard by W. T. Parke reflected the sentiments of these early day visitors. It was postmarked in 1905 and the writer "cannot imagine a more delightful place. My two weeks has been perfect." $20+ each.

Estes Park Village

Estes Park Village has been a haven for tourists since the 1870s when ranchers who settled in the area found that accommodating visitors provided a more lucrative income than raising cattle. At first they rented space in their homes, but eventually they began adding tents to their property, building additions, and opening new businesses to serve the growing number of tourists and locals. The town has grown over the years, but its main industry continues to be tourism.

7612. Estes Park Hotel, Estes Park, Colo.

Estes Park was named for Joel Estes who settled in the area with his family in 1860. A more colorful character was the Earl of Dunraven, who arrived in 1872. So taken with the surroundings, he came up with a plan to buy as much of the land as he could for his own hunting preserve. He hired an agent who arranged to pay people to file homestead claims. In exchange, Dunraven would purchase the land from the would-be settlers before the homestead requirements could be met. He had gained control of 15,000 acres before losing much of it when his scheme was uncovered. Dunraven started his plans for a hotel in Estes Park near what is now Fish Creek Road in 1874. It opened in 1877 under the name Dunraven's Estes Park Hotel. It was also known as the English Hotel. *Courtesy of the Estes Park Museum.*

View of the Estes Park Hotel showing the building after the second floor porch was removed and a wing was added to increase the number of guest rooms. Amenities included a nine-hole golf course, tennis courts, and a man-made lake. By this time Dunraven's holdings included the hotel, his personal home, a ranch house, stable, barn, dairy, and 6,600 acres. The remaining land was lost to new legal homesteaders. The Estes Park Development Company purchased the Dunraven holdings in 1908. The hotel was destroyed by an explosion and fire in 1911. Unmarked postcard, $20+.

15045. Town of Estes Park, Colorado.

The town site of Estes Park was platted in 1905 by C. H. Bond and encompassed the area around six buildings: the Cleave home; Parke's store; Miss Foot's Grocery; Sam Service's General Store and his home; and the school building. Sam Service moved to Estes Park in 1901 and built a building for his General Store in 1905. It offered an assortment of goods including groceries and construction supplies. This HHT Co. postcard shows the General Store across the road on the bottom right with an automobile parked in front. $20+.

Estes Park, Colo.

An early view of Estes Park thought to be Elkhorn Avenue before 1909. One of the many tent cabins in town is shown on the lower left. The message on the back of the card reads, "Went to a beautiful little berg – typical mountain town – just shacks – tents what they call houses. Where the 'X' is was a tent stretched over a frame with a board floor – makes a nice home – not so cold." Many tourists stayed in similar accommodations through the 1920s. $40+. Postcard by Barkalow Bros. Publishers, of Denver, Colorado. *Courtesy of the Colorado Collection/Estes Park Public Library*.

448—Panorama of
Estes Park Village
Mt. Olympus in Distance

Shown is an Estes Park street scene, looking westbound on Elkhorn Avenue. The Sherwood Hotel with its distinctive dormers is located beyond the church on the left. The hotel burned in 1956. Sanborn postcard, circa 1930s, $6-8.

D 3003. The Town of Estes Park, Colo.

This view was taken from west of Elkhorn Avenue looking to the east and showing the Manford Hotel with its covered porch, later called the Hupp Annex, at the top right. Sam Service's General Store is the white building on the lower right. Even though the area was growing, it had not yet become an official town. That changed when an election was held on April 3, 1917, and seventy-three of eighty-five voters cast ballots to begin incorporation. Following the voters' wishes, Estes Park became a full-fledged town on April 17, 1917. Postcard by W. T. Parke, of Estes Park, $25+.

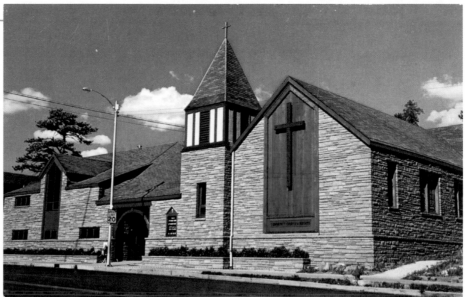

A brick facade was later added to the church. In 1982 a new church, now known as the Community Church of the Rockies, was built and the congregation moved to a twenty-six acre site north of the Estes Park Country Club. The church building on Elkhorn Avenue has been converted to house several gift shops under the name Old Church Shops. Postcard by Ray Surguine News Agency, of Boulder, Colorado, $3-5.

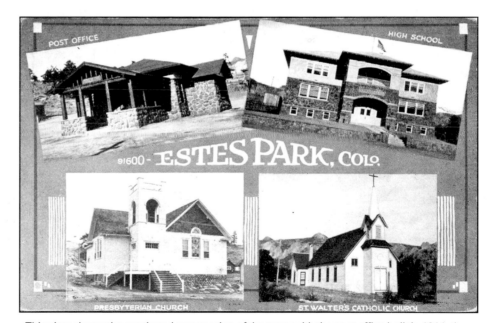

The first church built in Estes Park is shown in the lower left-hand corner of this Sanborn postcard. The land was purchased for $600 in 1907 with a loan from the Presbyterian Board of Missions. Volunteers built the church in 1909 at a cost of $4,000. The church was enlarged in 1935. Circa 1930s, $8-10.

This view shows the continued progression of the town with the post office built in 1914, the high school constructed in 1916, and St. Walter's Catholic Church, which was completed in 1915. This HHT Co. postcard reads, "The Town of Estes Park has developed rapidly within the past few years, and the residents take great pride in their public and church buildings." Circa 1920s, $25+.

91020. Trout Fishing in Rocky Mountain National Park.

Early fishermen like the one shown in this HHT Co. postcard appreciated what the Estes Park entrepreneurs had done to stock the area streams. $8-10.

13178. Federal Trout Hatcheries, Estes Park, Colo.

The Estes Park Protective and Improvement Association was organized in 1906 and plans were made to raise funds to build a fish hatchery to stock the area streams. It opened in July of 1907. By the 1920s, the state was operating the hatchery and a new facility was built. It continued in operation until it was destroyed by the Lawn Lake flood in 1982. An HHT Co. postcard, $15+.

GOLF CLUB - ESTES PARK.

The original Country Club building built in 1916 is still in use as the clubhouse for the Estes Park eighteen-hole public golf course. The Country Club was organized when thirty local investors formed the Estes Park Golf and Country Club. The course opened in 1917 with eighteen holes and sand greens. In 1944-45, the town of Estes Park acquired stock in the operation and later entered into a lease with the recreation district to develop a modern eighteen-hole course and remodel the log clubhouse. The golf course is one of the oldest in operation west of the Mississippi. A W. T. Parke postcard, $15+.

Ted Jelsema built the Dark Horse Tavern in 1933 after prohibition was repealed. The unusual bar seats were made from horses once used on a merry-go-round and named after famous western rodeo horses. The postcard describes the tavern as, "Nationally famous Dark Horse Bar, open all year operated in connection with the beautifully rustic Riverside Ballroom." Jelsema, along with Frank Bond, had built the Riverside Amusement Park circa 1922-23, which also included an outdoor swimming pool and a dance hall. After being used for other purposes, Riverside was sold to the town of Estes Park in 1969; the buildings were demolished in 1970 and the land was turned into parking lots. Postcard distributed by Clatworthy Colorvues, of Estes Park. Circa 1950s, $3-5.

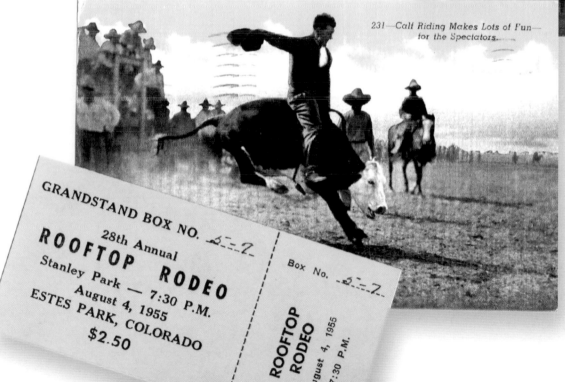

231—Calf Riding Makes Lots of Fun— for the Spectators.

GRANDSTAND BOX NO.

28th Annual
ROOFTOP RODEO
Stanley Park — 7:30 P.M.
August 4, 1955
ESTES PARK, COLORADO
$2.50

Box No.

ROOFTOP RODEO
August 4, 1955
7:30 P.M.

The Rooftop Rodeo at the Stanley Park Fairgrounds has been a favorite for western entertainment in Estes Park for decades and continues today. At an elevation of 7,500 feet, it was advertised as the highest rodeo competition in the country when the event was founded in 1941. Before the Rooftop Rodeo was organized, various bronco-busting contests were held in the town dating back to 1908. This Sanborn postcard was mailed from Estes Park during the inaugural summer of the Rooftop Rodeo. Also shown is a rodeo ticket from August, 1955. Postcard, $6-8; ticket, $5+.

The Historic Park Theatre is one of the most visible of the Estes Park landmarks. Construction began in 1913 by J. L. Jackson and was completed in 1914 by C. H. Bond. The property was then sold to Fred Jackson, who operated it as a theatre for silent films. In 1922, Ralph Gwynn, a theater projectionist from Denver, bought the property and added an eighty-foot tower named "Tower of Love" in 1926 to the one-story building, making it the tallest structure in the area. Ola and Richard Stanger purchased the theatre in 1982. The business is said to be the oldest motion picture theatre in operation west of the Mississippi River. Photo by Clatworthy Jr. *Courtesy of the Historic Park Theatre*.

Because of its tall tower, Park Theatre can easily be seen from most anywhere near the downtown business district. The tower's neon lights are permitted to be illuminated at night following approval from Estes Park residents in a special vote in 1984; that same year, it was placed on the National Register of Historic Places. Sanborn postcard, $4-6.

ELK IN ESTES PARK

Before 1900, elk were plentiful in the Estes Park-Rocky Mountain National Park region. But by 1910 after homesteaders, tourists, and workers had settled in the area, the elk herds were depleted. It was only after the herd was lost that the Estes Park businessmen realized how valuable the elk had been as a tourist attraction. They soon arranged for a reintroduction program and in 1913 small herds of twenty-five Yellowstone elk were moved by rail from Montana to nearby Lyons. From there, they were transported to Moraine Park and other locations. The plan worked and was described in an article in the *Estes Park Trail* on September 22, 1922, in which a single herd of fifty-six elk had been sighted in Horseshoe Park. This W. T. Parke postcard image was used by the newspaper to illustrate the report. $15+.

The reintroduction plan worked so well that elk in the area have proliferated far beyond the early townspeople's expectation. Although elk are still abundant in Rocky Mountain National Park, they are also making themselves at home in unexpected locations, including parks, golf courses, and residents' yards. Pictured are a dozen elk taking a break in Bond Park along Elkhorn Avenue on a busy summer afternoon. While the elk population has grown too large in the national park, it is a problem that has become difficult to address given the conflicts associated with the issue.

Lake Estes' Olympus Dam saved the town from catastrophic damage during the Lawn Lake flood on July 15, 1982. The lake had been made years earlier as a result of the Colorado-Big Thompson project that brought water from the west at Grand Lake through a tunnel to the east. The water was collected behind Olympus Dam to form the lake, taking from 1938 to 1957 to complete. Much of the land covered by the 185-acre lake was once part of the holdings of Lord Dunraven. Lake Estes postcard by J. A. Ossen Co., of Denver, Colorado, $3-5.

299 Lawn Lake and Mt. Fairchilds, Estes Park, Colo.

A breach in the Lawn Lake Dam sent floodwaters into Estes Park during the short but destructive flood of 1982. The lake was located in Rocky Mountain National Park, but before it became part of the park a group of Loveland businessmen formed the Farmer's Irrigation Ditch & Reservoir Company and enlarged the lake. After the lake became part of the park, the dam was no longer maintained. Because of this lack of maintenance, a leaking outlet pipe damaged the dam's structure. The dam broke on July 15 and the escaping water poured into the Roaring River, then into Cascade Lake. This caused a breach in the Cascade Dam, sending the water down Fall River, and eventually making its way to Elkhorn Avenue. The floodwater then joined Big Thompson River and flowed into Lake Estes. The Olympus Dam at the edge of Lake Estes held and the floodwaters were stopped. While the flood lasted just four hours, three campers were killed and many businesses were damaged. A W.T. Parke postcard, $8-10.

KINNIKINNIK MOTOR HOTEL, *Nothing finer*, ESTES PARK, COLORADO

LOCATED IN THE HEART OF THE WORLD'S FINEST VACATION LAND

By the late 1950s and early 1960s, tourists and tourism began to change in Estes Park and Rocky Mountain National Park. Tourists were traveling longer distances and spending only a couple of days in the park. Motels like the Kinnikinnik Motor Hotel, located one mile south of Estes Park on Highway 7, were opened to accommodate this new kind of tourist. Postcard by Clatworthy Colorvue, of Estes Park, $10+.

Many thought new attractions were needed to serve the faster paced tourists of the 1950s. To meet that demand, the Estes Park Aerial Tramway was opened in 1955. It includes two ten-passenger cabins that carry tramway passengers to the summit of Prospect Mountain. Sanborn postcard, $3-5. Also pictured is a tram souvenir, $20+.

KOA CAMPGROUND
ESTES PARK, COLORADO

Although there had been tent campers for decades, it wasn't until the 1950s that camping out on vacations became more prevalent. When travel trailers and pop-up campers were added to the mix, additional campgrounds were needed to meet the demand. This postcard from David Hallacy Color Brochures, of Denver, shows the KOA Estes Park campground, which is still in business today. Circa 1964, $6-8.

Lodges/Hotels

For more than one hundred years, the hoteliers of Estes Park have welcomed guests with unsurpassed hospitality. Long-lasting friendships were formed between the innkeepers and their repeat customers during these summer visits, and today, many of the children and grandchildren of those earlier visitors make the pilgrimage to Estes Park to experience that same friendly hospitality and scenic beauty.

Hupp and Manford Hotels

D 3002. The Manford Hotel, Estes Park, Colo.

No. 266. The Hupp, Long's Peak in distance, Estes Park, Colo.

The Manford Hotel opened in June 1908 with guest rooms to accommodate fifty people. John Manford's hotel was located at the corner of Elkhorn Avenue and Big Horn Drive. As reported in the *Mountaineer* on June 11, 1908, the lower floor included a large dining room, ladies' parlor, men's smoking rooms, and office. The upper floor contained guest rooms. The hotel was sold later that year to Josephine Hupp and it became the Hupp Annex. $25+. *Courtesy of the Colorado Collection/Estes Park Public Library*.

Josephine Hupp built her first hotel called the Hupp in 1906. It was located on the southwest corner of Elkhorn and Moraine avenues and later became known as the Estes Park Hotel. The Indian Village Trading Post now occupies the space. This W. T. Parke postcard was postmarked 1909. $30+.

464   THE HUPP HOTEL, ESTES PARK, COLO.

ROCKY MOUNTAIN NATIONAL PARK, COLO.

2258-30

The Hupp Hotel (originally Manford/Hupp Annex) as it looked in 1931 after several changes of ownership. Stucco had been added to the original wood, the porches were removed, shops were housed on the first floor, and additions had been added. Today, it houses a number of businesses. Sanborn postcard, $15+.

400.   VILLAGE OF ESTES PARK.

ROCKY MOUNTAIN NATIONAL PARK, COLORADO.

108255

Josephine Hupp established a varied and successful career in hotel ownership from 1906 until 1930. This Sanborn postcard shows several of the Hupp hotels along Elkhorn Avenue. No. 1 is the original Hupp Hotel, now the Indian Trading Post. No. 2 is the Manford Hotel-Hupp Annex-Hupp Hotel. No. 3 is the Josephine Hotel-Riverside Hotel-Wheel Bar. Hupp built the Josephine Hotel in 1916, sold it to the Lewiston Hotel Co. circa 1920, and bought it back in 1926. In 1930 it was purchased by Ted Jelsema and became the Riverside Hotel. The hotel was severely damaged by fire in 1956. The first floor was saved and is still in use. The Wheel Bar has been located in the building since 1945. No. 4 is the Sherwood Hotel, purchased by Hupp in 1923. It was located east of the church on Elkhorn Avenue and burned in 1956. $8-10.

91199

BROWN TEA POT INN
ESTES PARK,
COLORADO.

The Brown Tea Pot was located a few buildings to the east of the Community Church on Elkhorn Avenue. Mrs. L. L. Norton successfully operated it for many years. In 1915 Norton added a three-story hotel to her building. This 25-room hotel eventually became the Sherwood Hotel later operated by Josephine Hupp. An HHT Co. postcard, $25+.
Courtesy of David Scarbrough, Mountain Time.

The James family also built cabins like the one shown in the foreground of this post-card. A similar structure behind the main lodge was used as the first Estes Park School. Classes were held on the Elkhorn property for several years beginning in 1883-84 until a new school was built at the northwest corner of Moraine and Elkhorn avenues. An F. P. Clatworthy postcard, $25+.

William and Ella James and their family moved to Estes Park in 1875. In 1877 they built a home by Fall River with plans to run a cattle ranch. The family, like most early Estes Park settlers, discovered tourism was more profitable. They began adding rooms to their house to provide space for visitors. The lodge and its surrounding two hundred acres was named Elkhorn because of the elk in the area. Shown in the postcard's foreground is the lodge as it looked in the early 1900s. It combined the original barn and the ranch house to make a larger structure. When William James died in 1895, his son Homer left his medical practice to help run the lodge. In the early 1900s, a new Elkhorn Lodge was built on the property, as shown in the postcard's background. This lodge booklet circa early 1900s, describes the new lodge: "The buildings consist of the New Hotel; the Old Lodge; a casino; ten cottages, livery stable, and laundry. It has spacious verandas, smoking room, and a dining hall. The casino contains a dance-hall, billiard room, and barber shop." Postcard, $30+; booklet, $60+. Postcard by Barkalow Bros. Publishers, of Denver, Colorado. *Postcard courtesy of the Colorado Collection/Estes Park Public Library.*

By the 1920s, Elkhorn Lodge had been enlarged once again to provide additional lodging to house its many guests. $40. *Courtesy of the Colorado Collection/Estes Park Public Library.*

The inside of the Elkhorn Lodge is shown in this hand-colored postcard published by the Albertype Co. The original furnishings include several pieces of early Stickley mission furniture. Although both Ella James and her son Howard had passed away by the end of the 1920s, younger family members continued to operate the lodge until it was sold in 1961. During the James family tenure, guests were entertained with horseback rides, picnics, bingo, card games, fishing, swimming, and square dancing in the later years. Because of the long tenure of the James family, the Elkhorn Lodge became the oldest operating tourist facility in Estes Park. $30+. *Courtesy of David Scarbrough, Mountain Time.*

Flatiron postcard of lodge. Six of the Elkhorn lodge buildings constructed from 1877 to 1908 were added to the National Register of Historical Places in 1978. They include the original lodge on the lower right, which was made by joining the ranch house and the barn, and the newer lodge built circa early 1900s, center. Also included on the list but not pictured is a cabin with a bay window built in 1886, said to have been used for church services in the early days; and a pair of two-storied framed structured guest houses called "A" and "B" with porches on their south sides, both built in 1908. Circa 1950s, $15+.

The Rustic Hotel, Estes Park, Colo.

The Rustic Hotel was opened in 1901 and was located at the north end of Estes Park near the head of Devils Gulch. The owner was Shepherd Husted who later became a famous guide in the Estes area. Husted eventually encountered financial difficulties, resulting in the hotel being purchased by Charles E. Lester in 1913. Lester had been managing Dunraven's Estes Park Hotel until it burned in 1911. A W. T. Parke postcard, $30+.

91023-LESTERS HOTEL, ESTES PARK
R.M.N.P

Under the new ownership, the Rustic Hotel was renamed Lester's Hotel. In 1921 the complex included a main building, ten cottages, and a large dining room. The drawing room, smoking room, writing room, and library were located in the main building. The hotel offered tennis courts, croquet, riding, fishing, and golf parties. In 1933 Lester sold the hotel to Julian Livingston and it was renamed the H Bar G Ranch. The facility operated as a dude ranch through 1958 and was then used for a variety of purposes including a girl's camp, housing for a Youth Conservation Corps, and a youth hostel. It is now a private facility. For more information on Estes Park lodges and hotels, consult *Those Castles of Wood* by Henry F. Pedersen. An HHT Co. postcard, $30+.

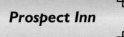

Prospect Inn was built in 1915. It included a dining room, large lobby, and seven bedrooms. The inn was located on Park Lane near the Elkhorn Avenue downtown district. In 1919, owner Mrs. S. M. Spanier listed the capacity of the inn at thirty people who paid from $2 to $2.50 a day. After several owners, the inn was sold in 1978 to Gary R. Brown who converted it into office space and renamed it the Park Lane Building. Sanborn postcard, $20+.

National Park Hotel

The National Park Hotel on Elkhorn Avenue was opened in 1919 by Harriet Byerly and continued to operate until the early 1970s with family members taking over upon Byerly's death in 1955. The building was then sold and converted into a Ripley's Believe It or Not Museum where it attracted curious visitors for nearly a decade. The building now houses a collection of shops. Sanborn postcard, $40+.

Olympus Lodge

Olympus Lodge was named for the mountain on Estes Park's east boundary. It was built in 1923 to be the mountain school of the Colorado State Teachers College in Greeley. The Camp Olympus programs included classes in natural history. The summer mountain school for educators was quite popular in the 1920s and 1930s. The lodge and the other remaining assets were sold to W. Earl Hope in 1951. In 1952 the third story was removed from the lodge; twelve motel units and seven two-bedroom cabins replaced the lost space. The lodge continues to operate today. Sanborn postcard showing Olympus Lodge at right, circa 1940s, $20+.

The Estes Park Land and Investment Company built Wind River Lodge in 1902. It was a two-story rustic structure containing fourteen rooms. Additional buildings and cabins were also constructed on the property. In 1908 the YMCA (Young Men's Christian Association) developed a Western Conference and purchased the Wind River Lodge as well as 334 acres in 1910 from the original owners. This was the initial investment that would eventually become the YMCA of the Rockies, located five miles southwest of Estes Park. Photograph by F. P. Clatworthy, hand-colored by Cheryl Pennington. *Courtesy of the Lula W. Dorsey Museum.*

Additional buildings were soon added to the YMCA property. Included was a new Dining and Social Hall using "Western Stick" architecture built in 1910. It was designed by Thomas P. Barber of Colorado Springs and later became the Administration Building. To learn more, refer to the book, *YMCA of the Rockies*, by Jack R. Melton and Lulabeth Melton. An HHT Co. postcard, $10+.

The YMCA conference grounds are shown on this Phostint Detroit Publishing postcard. The depression years were difficult for the YMCA. At one point the financial situation looked so bleak, it began negotiations to sell the property to the Park Service, but the deal never materialized. By 1938, with stricter budgets and more focus on young people's athletic and church groups, the organization had one of its best seasons. Circa 1917, $8-10.

Mountainside Lodge was completed in 1920 to be used as a summer home for Dr. John Timothy Stone, a Chicago minister. When the home was sold in 1924, it was used as a lodge, a camp for girls, and a hotel. It was purchased by the YMCA in 1956 and became a setting for family reunions and church retreats. After years of neglect, renovation of the lodge began in 2005. Sanborn postcard, $15+.

Shown is the Lula W. Dorsey Museum on the grounds of the YMCA. The building includes the west end of Wind River Lodge, which was moved from its original location to become part of the museum and opened in 1979. With seven lodges and 206 family cabins over 860 acres, the YMCA is one of the top three attractions in the area and can accommodate up to 3,500 guests.

LONG'S PEAK

LONG'S PEAK INN, ESTES PARK, COLORADO

Enos Mills came to Estes Park in 1884 at the age of fourteen and soon built a homestead cabin. His first job was as a dishwasher at the Elkhorn Lodge. He later worked for his uncle, Elkanna Lamb, who owned Longs Peak House in the Tahosa Valley south of Estes Park. In 1902 Mills purchased his uncle's lodge and called it Longs Peak Inn. While the lodge was closed in the winter, Mills focused on his growing writing and lecturing career as a naturalist and accomplished photographer. *Courtesy of the Enos Mills Cabin.*

Shown is Longs Peak Inn shortly after Mills acquired the property. After a fire destroyed the inn in 1906, Mills began rebuilding the lodge using materials from the surrounding forest to fashion a unique rustic design. He was able to feed his guests in the new dining room by the Fourth of July of the same year. Located at the foot of Longs Peak, the inn specialized in providing guests with guides to help them climb to the summit. Mills initially led the trips, but as he became more involved in his naturalist role, which also included lobbying for the creation of Rocky Mountain National Park, he hired other guides, including Shep Husted. $8-10.

Longs Peak Inn as it looked after being rebuilt in 1906, although this postcard dates from a later period. The lodge building included a living room, dining room, post office and bookstore, and a nature room for talks and exhibits. Mills did not allow card playing or dancing in his establishment. Guests were encouraged to focus their activities on nature, symbolic of the inn's rustic architecture. Additional cabins were built from 1909-1916. Postcard by Pictorial Postals, of New York City, $15+.

Although most guests at Longs Peak Inn focused on Enos Mills as a naturalist, author, and lecturer, other aspects of his life are noteworthy. In 1918, he married Esther Burnell who had homesteaded in Estes Park two years earlier. The couple had a daughter named Enda. She is shown with her father in front of his homestead cabin. It was placed on the National Register of Historic Places in 1973 and can be visited by appointment. Enos died in 1922 shortly after this photograph was taken. According to his obituary in the *Estes Park Trail*, he died of complications from a series of lingering medical conditions stemming from a subway accident that occurred the preceding winter. *The Trail's* obituary identified Mills as "the father of the Rocky Mountain National Park, the most popular National Park in America today." *Courtesy of the Enos Mills Cabin.*

Mills' guests politely described the furniture at Longs Peak Inn as "unique." Some of the tables were held up with tree trunks as pictured in this postcard of the living room. The clerk's desk was also made from the trunk of a tree. $8-10.

LIVING ROOM, LONGS PEAK INN   Estes Park, Colo.

THE LOBBY, LONG'S PEAK INN, LONGS PEAK, COLORADO

A promotional postcard from 1919 shows the lobby of Longs Peak Inn and its unusual staircase and tree supports. The author of the card writes, "Enos A. Mills, the naturalist and author, is the proprietor of the inn and lives here all the time. I hate to leave here. I am sure California cannot compare with Estes Park. The mountains are wonderful and well named Rocky." Like this visitor, most of the guests enjoyed the atmosphere at the inn and the presence of professors, writers, and artists, which gave it an intellectual atmosphere. $8-10.

DINING ROOM, LONGS PEAK INN   Estes Park, Colo.

The dining room of Longs Peak Inn as it looked in 1911. Many pieces of hand-made rustic furniture can be seen. No tipping was allowed at the inn, which was emphasized in a 1920s brochure that referred to the lodge as "The Non-Tip House." $8-10.

NATURE BOOKS
The Grizzly
Wild Life on the Rockies
In Beaver World
The Spell of the Rockies
Adventures of a Nature Guide
Rocky Mountain Wonderland
Waiting in the Wilderness
Your National Parks
Watched by Wild Animals
The Story of Scotch
Wild Animal Homesteads
The Story of a Thousand Year Pine
The Rocky Mountain National Park
By ENOS A. MILLS

Shown is a Longs Peak Inn brochure. It includes photographs, maps, and tourist information, including recommended attire, such as "woolen knickers and hose, stout shoes, winter underwear, flannel shirt, hat, sweater, knapsack, and colored glasses." Esther Mills continued to operate the inn until 1945 when she sold the property. Circa late 1920s, $35+.

After Enos Mills' death, wife Esther was faced with running the inn and raising their daughter alone. When Enda was seven, Esther hired Patience Carins (later Kemp), daughter of early Grand Lake businessman James Cairns, as her daughter's summer companion. Shown are the two girls as they looked that summer. They began a friendship that lasted many years. *From the collection of Jane Kemp.*

71792   LONG'S PEAK AND LONG'S PEAK INN, ROCKY MTN. NAT'L PARK, COLORADO

Longs Peak Inn was destroyed by fire in 1949 and a new inn was built on the property, which was named Swiss Village. Bob and Virginia Akins purchased the property in 1972, restored the name, and refurbished the buildings. It was sold to the Salvation Army in 1991 and added to its High Peak Camp acreage. Esther Mills died in 1964 leaving as her survivors her daughter Enda Mills Kiley and granddaughter Elizabeth M. Mills Kiley. A great-granddaughter Eryn Mills Kiley has since been born into the family. Phostint postcard by Detroit Publishing Co., $15+.

Freelan Oscar Stanley was born in Kingfield, Maine, in 1849. He and his twin brother, Francis Edgar, invented the Stanley Steamer automobile that was sold from 1901 to 1924. The brothers also invented a photographic dry plate that was so successful, they made their fortunes when they sold that business in 1903 to George Eastman (Kodak). F. O. Stanley was in poor health with tuberculosis by the age of fifty-three and was sent to Colorado to see if the climate could help him recover. In the summer of 1903 he drove his Stanley Steamer from Denver to Estes Park, a feat no one had ever accomplished. He and his wife stayed at the Elkhorn Lodge for three months where he made a remarkable recovery before returning to Massachusetts. This photo shows F. O. Stanley in his 1903 Stanley Model B on a residential street in Massachusetts. Researchers believe this may be the same automobile that was shipped to Denver to be driven to Estes Park in June 1903. *Courtesy of the Stanley Museum, Kingfield, Maine*.

7487. Stanley Hotel, Estes Park, Colo.

7489. Auto Road, Estes Park, Colo.

In the fall of 1903 Stanley began building a Georgian-style home on the north side of Wonder View Avenue that was finished in 1904 and is still in use as a private residence. He purchased land from Lord Dunraven and began work on the Stanley Hotel in 1907. The Georgian-style hotel opened two years later. To supply electricity, Stanley built Cascade Dam across Fall River to power his new hydro plant's turbine. He also allowed others to use the electricity for a small fee. A water system was also constructed. The new hotel was three stories tall and cost $500,000 to construct. All rooms included private baths and telephones. The hotel also featured an unusual all-electric kitchen. Circa 1911, $20+. *Courtesy David Scarbrough, Mountain Time*.

In addition to his innovations that made for a better water supply and electricity, Stanley also contributed to the improvement of area roads to support his Estes Park Transportation Company, which was formed to provide touring buses to bring guests to the hotel from the train stations at Loveland and Lyons. Stanley sold his transportation company to Roe Emery in 1916. "Auto Road, Estes Park" postcard by HHT Co., $8-10.

Another building was added to the Stanley enterprise when the Stanley Manor was built in 1910. It included thirty-three rooms, as well as its own dining room, parlor, and billiard room. Later a casino was added to the property. It could seat six hundred people for concerts and included a basement with a bowling alley. A large garage was also constructed on the property, which provided automobile storage. $10+.

15185. Stanley Hotels, Estes Park, Colorado, Rocky Mountain National Park.

ROCKY MOUNTAIN NATIONAL — ESTES PARK, COLORADO
— A VERITABLE SUMMER PARADISE FOR FOLKS OF ALL AGES.
Burlington Route — Direct to the Park.

In addition to entertainment for adults, the Stanley also offered recreation for children. There was a playground with swings and slides, and a croquet course as shown on this Burlington Route Railroad postcard. The Stanley Livery also provided horseback riding that was located off the grounds. $6-8.

The Stanley Hotel was sold to Roe Emery and his Rocky Mountain Motor Co. in 1929. The hotel was furnished with traditional furniture made of mahogany in keeping with its architecture. The hotel also featured unique woodwork using special designs made of plaster. Dances remained popular at the Stanley, especially during the Big Band era. Emery's firm operated the hotel until 1946, while the Stanleys used their Estes Park vacation home for many more years. Stanley's wife Flora died in the home at the age of ninety-three. Stanley passed away the next year in Newton, Massachusetts, when he was ninety-one. Sanborn postcard, $6-8.

Shown is a brochure for the Stanley Hotel after the Abbell Management Company had acquired it. The once exclusive hotel is represented with a western theme, perhaps to attract the more down-to-earth tourist after World War II. The hotel had been closed during most of the war. Circa 1949, $20+. *Courtesy of the Stanley Museum of Colorado.*

In 1977 the Stanley Hotel and its buildings was listed on the National Register of Historic Places. By the late 1970s and 1980s, the hotel went through some rough times and was nearly set for demolition until the Colorado Historical Society saved it. Since the 1990s the Stanley Hotel has been under new ownership when it was purchased and renovated by John Cullen. After one hundred years F. O. Stanley's dream has continued to endure. Hotel swimming pool postcard by Dexter Press, $3-5.

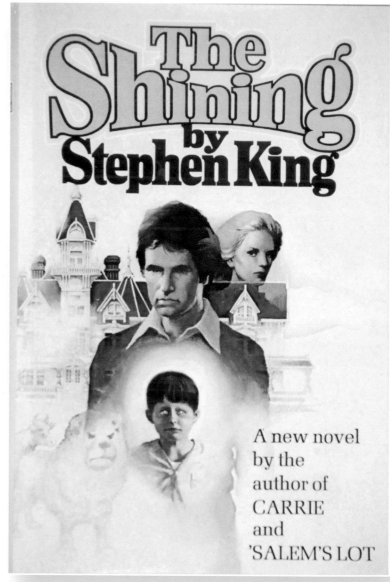

Today, many of the hotel's guests and visitors are attracted to the Stanley because of the popularity of Stephen King's book, movie, and mini-series, *The Shining*, which is based on the hotel. In 1973 King developed the basic plot for his third novel while visiting the hotel during a trip to Estes Park. While the film made from the book was shot elsewhere, the later mini-series shown on ABC in 1997 was filmed at the hotel. Shown is a copy of King's *The Shining*, published by Doubleday, copyright 1977. $10.

Voelkel's Glacier Lodge had its beginning in 1894 when the original homestead was built by Colorado Governor James Peabody. In 1912 Cora, the governor's daughter, and her husband Grover Voelkel opened the property as Voelkel's Glacier Lodge. This Christmas card features the lodge and the signature of the owners, Cora and Grover. Circa 1940s, $35+.

Shown is the lodge, the dining room, and the nearby Big Thompson River. It is labeled "The Switzerland of America." The lodge is located 3.5 miles southwest of Estes Park on Highway 66. $35+. *Courtesy of David Scarbrough, Mountain Time.*

A Sanborn postcard of the lodge buildings as they looked circa 1930s. The Voelkels operated the lodge for sixty years until they sold it to Penne and Jim Ranglos in 1974 and the name of the property was shortened to Glacier Lodge. $25+. *Courtesy of David Scarbrough, Mountain Time.*

A Sanborn postcard of the knotty pine dining room at the lodge during Voelkel's ownership. A large fireplace is included in the room. $35+.

A view of the lodge buildings as they looked in the 1950s showing the main lodge and dining room. The main lodge has been renovated and is still used as one of the many buildings housing guests. Two generations of Ranglos family members have spent over thirty years adding thirty-four cabins of various sizes, a recreation hall, and other buildings to the twenty-acre property. Dave and Karen Ranglos began operating the lodge in 1996. Sanborn Souvenir Co. postcard, $10+.

THE CRAGS

Crags Hotel opened for business in 1914. It was built by Enoch "Joe" Mills, brother of naturalist Enos Mills. It is located on the north slope of Prospect Mountain south of Estes Park and was named Crags because it was built into the craggy part of the mountain. This postcard dates from its early days. $35+. *Courtesy of the Colorado Collection/Estes Park Public Library.*

THE CRAGS HOTEL.   ESTES PARK, COLORADO.   *Aug. 6.*

The Crags as it looked after Mills and his wife Ethel had enlarged the lodge in the early 1920s. Fifty new guest rooms were added and the dining room could then seat three hundred people. Mills had also been a college professor, but by 1924 he turned his attention to running the lodge and writing and lecturing about nature full-time. Cabins and a recreation hall were soon added to the lodge. Like his brother before him, Joe Mills died at an early age when his automobile collided with a Denver tram car in 1935. Hand-colored postcard by F. P. Clatworthy. $25+.

THE
Crags
ESTES PARK
COLORADO

"The Friendly House on the Hill"

The Crags dining room showing the Old Hickory furniture that was delivered to the lodge by horse and carriage for its 1914 opening and is still in use today. Other pieces of hickory furniture have been added to the lodge's furnishings through the years. Postcard by Colorado Specta-Vues, of Arapaho Valley Ranch, Granby, Colorado, $8-10.

Ethel Mills continued to operate the Crags until 1946 when it was sold to Ralph and Hazel Reed. "The Friendly House on the Hill" was owned and operated by one or more members of the Reed family for the next several decades. This brochure using the familiar slogan was produced during this tenure. It includes an added insert announcing a new swimming pool that was to be opened that summer. $25+.

This unusual Crags postcard shows the lodge from a different angle so its various buildings can be seen. The property received a makeover in 1978 and cabins were moved to prepare land for home sites. The lodge itself has become a timeshare property that includes rentals when available. It is listed on the National Register of Historic Places. Sanborn postcard, $5-8.

The Lewiston Hotel was developed by A. D. "Gus" Lewis who moved to Estes in 1912 to work at the Estes Park Bank. He built a house in 1914 and began renting rooms to tourists. In 1915 he added on to his home so he could house more guests. By 1917 he had raised the height of the building so seventy guests could be accommodated. This early W. T. Parke postcard shows the Lewiston Hotel circa 1917. It stood on a rocky knoll overlooking Estes Park. $30+.

Alpha Kappa

FIFTH
ANNUAL
DANCE

LEWISTON HOTEL
Estes Park, Colo.

May twenty-third
Nineteen Twenty-five

Lewis continued to enlarge his hotel in 1918-1919 when it was expanded to three stories. The hotel could by then handle 150 guests. This hand-colored postcard by F. P. Clatworthy shows the Lewiston as it looked in its prime. Also pictured is an Alpha Kappa program from a dance held there in 1925. Lewis also built the Lewiston Chalets and Grand Lake Lodge, which he sold in 1923. Other hotels owned by Lewis were the Josephine, and the Lewiston Café and Rooms. Postcard, $25+; program, $10+.

Only the Stanley Hotel rivaled the Lewiston Hotel in its grandeur. The Lewiston included a lobby, main lounge, ballroom, billiard and game room, and a spacious dining room. Sanborn postcard, $8-10.

ROCKY MOUNTAIN NATIONAL PARK, COLORADO   116969

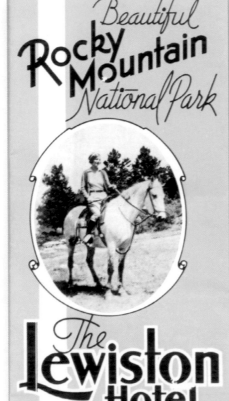

This Lewiston folder dates from the early 1930s. Guests had access to horses with special trips arranged. Prices ranged from $5 to $6.50 per day. There were also tennis courts, golf, and swimming within a few minutes drive. $35+.

The Lewiston Hotel was nearing the end of its season on September 4, 1941, with the staff preparing for a conference banquet when a fire began in a flue in the attic. The wind was blowing fiercely and the flames spread quickly once they reached the roof. The hotel's hilltop location, as shown in this view, hampered firefighters from getting their hoses close to the building. *The Estes Park Trail* estimated the loss at $300,000. All that remains of the Lewiston today is a stone wall on the hill at the west end of Elkhorn Avenue. F. P. Clatworthy hand-colored postcard, $25+.

The Baldpate Inn, owned and operated by Gordon and Ethel Mace, opened seven miles south of Estes Park in 1917. Unlike many of the local lodges of the period, the new seven-room structure included electricity and indoor plumbing. A dance hall and casino were added to the property in 1921. Hand-colored postcard published for Baldpate Inn by the Albertype Co., of Brooklyn, New York, $8-10.

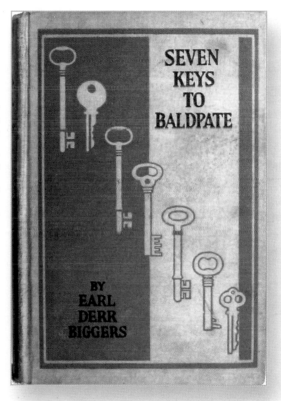

The name of the new inn came from a popular mystery book of the day called *Seven Keys to Baldpate* by Earl Derr Biggers. Shown is a copy of the book published by Grosset and Dunlap/ The Bobbs-Merrill Co., copyright 1913. *Courtesy of Jane Kemp.*

The Maces used the "key" theme in their advertising by placing keys on the seven mile posts between Estes and the inn. Many motorists, like these pictured circa 1918, were surprised to discover the signs led to the unique inn and were inclined to stop for lunch. $30+.

The owners continued the inn's theme by giving each guest a key when they checked out. This tradition ended because of its cost, but the guests had already begun a custom of their own by sending back interesting keys they owned. These keys became so numerous that in 1935 a "key room" was designed to hold the collection. An estimated 20,000 keys have been added over the years. The inn continues to receive about two hundred keys a year from its guests from all over the world. Hand-colored postcard by the Albertype Co., of Brooklyn, New York, published for the inn, $8-10.

The "Seven Keys to Baldpate Inn" hung on a large key ring on its two-story porch for many years. This hand-colored postcard was also published for Baldpate Inn by the Albertype Co. of Brooklyn, New York, $8-10.

A promotional brochure for Baldpate Inn. The owners describe their inn as "roughing it with a degree of comfort," and add that there are "few restrictions at Baldpate which, fortunately, houses a class which makes obvious rules and regulations unnecessary." Circa 1920s, $35+.

BALDPATE INN

Estes

Rocky Mountain National Park

Postcard featuring the inn's guest lounge in earlier days. Some pieces of the hickory furniture are still in use on the veranda. Postcard by Albertype Co., of Brooklyn, New York, $25. *Courtesy of The Baldpate Inn, Ltd.*

Dance Tonight

Baldpate Casino

ADMISSION: FIFTY CENTS EACH PERSON

Shown is a ticket to a dance at the Baldpate Dance Hall and Casino, circa 1920s. It was located across the road from the main lodge. The building collapsed due to the weight of heavy snows in the early 1980s, according to information supplied by owner Lois Smith. The fireplace was preserved and a sun deck and outdoor stage have been made with materials salvaged from some of the dance floor. *Courtesy of the Baldpate Inn, Ltd.*

The Baldpate Inn was purchased by Mike and Lois Smith in 1986. The Smiths reopened the dining room to the public and operate the inn as a bed and breakfast. The owners take pride in the museum quality of the inn, which, in addition to its collection of keys, displays many old photographs and all of the original guest books. The inn was added to the National Register of Historic Places in 1996. Shown is an old Baldpate Inn room key. *Courtesy of the Baldpate Inn, Ltd.*

Columbine Lodge was built by Harry Bitner circa 1908 in the Tahosa Valley nine miles south of Estes Park. After several changes of ownership, it was purchased by Charles Alexander in 1916 and he continued to run the business until 1944. The lodge was built near Longs Peak Inn, and in addition to the lodge building, the property included a dining hall and rustic cabins. Sanborn postcard, $20. *Courtesy of David Scarbrough, Mountain Time*.

A Columbine Lodge promotional brochure issued by C. H. Alexander, proprietor. Circa 1920s, $55+.

Shown is the inside of Columbine Lodge. It was furnished with rustic hickory furniture along with colorful Indian rugs. The lodge is now called High Peak Camp and is owned by the Salvation Army for use as a camp for inner-city youth. $30+. *Courtesy of David Scarbrough, Mountain Time*.

The McGraw Ranch was purchased in 1884 by Peter J. Pauly Jr. from an earlier homesteader. It was located six miles north of Estes Park. Pauly sold the ranch in 1897 to Hugo Miller, who then sold it to John and Irene McGraw circa 1909. Several years after John's death, the ranch was converted to a dude ranch in the mid 1930s. Recreational activities included horseback riding, fishing, pack trips, and steak fries. The ranch continued in business until the 1970s when it was sold. Circa 1945, $25+.

By 1988 the National Park Service had acquired the McGraw Ranch holdings. The ranch house and the other historic buildings on the property have since been restored to provide housing for researchers. These residents study various flora and fauna species in the park and share their research in exchange for free accommodations. The ranch is on the National Register of Historic Places. This postcard is labeled "McGraw Ranch, Estes Park, Colo. Gov. Landon's Summer Vacation Home." Circa late 1930s, $25. *Courtesy of David Scarbrough, Mountain Time.*

The Cheley Colorado Camps, Estes Park, Colo.

The popular Cheley Colorado Camps had their beginning in the early 1920s at Bear Lake when Frank H. Cheley began a camp for boys. A girls camp was started in 1926 near the YMCA property. With their success, Cheley purchased land four miles south of Estes Park and moved both camps to the new property in 1927. Cheley Colorado Camps Trading Post postcard, circa 1934, $35+. *Courtesy of David Scarbrough, Mountain Time.*

Cheley Colorado Camps brochure for the 1934 season. Prices ranged from $35 per week for the Junior Camp, to $45 per week for the older boys and girls. The facilities included all permanent buildings, hot showers, dining lodge, recreation buildings, stables, infirmary, rifle range, tennis courts, and outdoor swimming pool. Founder Frank Cheley died in 1941 and his son Jack continued to manage the camps. Currently Jack's son Donald and his family are in charge of the camps. $35+.

GIRLS LODGE, CHELEY, CAMPS

This earlier postcard shows the "Girls Lodge" after the boys and girls camps were moved to new facilities south of Estes Park. Circa late 1920s, $40+. *Courtesy of David Scarbrough collection.*

Estes Park Surroundings

In addition to the lodges in Estes Park, guest facilities in the surrounding areas were popular as well. Included were those in Glen Haven and Drake to the northeast, reached by Devils Gulch and Big Thompson Canyon on U.S. Highway 34; and Meeker Park and Allenspark to the south on Highway 7. Most of these stops included dining facilities for travelers.

Meeker Park Lodge

Meeker Park Lodge, located south of Estes Park on Highway 7, was constructed in 1929 as part of a larger resort that included rental cabins. Two couples from nearby Longmont were the owners: Danny Dever, his wife Crete, and H. Gay and Leota Nowels. After Leota's death, her husband left the business. This postcard shows the lodge, which included a dining room, a small store, and gas pumps. Sanborn postcard, circa 1940s, $30+.

This postcard of the lodge in the 1950s states, "Friendly atmosphere. Western-style lodge. One of the most visited resorts at the foot of 13,911 ft. Mt. Meeker – adjoining the Rocky Mountain Nat'l Park." The younger members of the Dever family took over management of the lodge with the passing of Danny and the aging of Crete. Meeker Park Lodge continues to operate after over eighty-five years in business. $20+.

Hewes-Kirkwood Inn opened circa 1913 with Mary Kirkwood and her sons Charles and Steve Hewes as owners. Although it had its beginning as Mary Kirkwood's cabin, which was located close to Longs Peak Trail near what is now Highway 7, the cabin was enlarged and new buildings were added to form the final resort. It consisted of the lodge building, a dining room in its own facility, at least a dozen cabins, a laundry, stable, work shop, and employee housing. Circa 1920s, $30+. *Courtesy of David Scarbrough, Mountain Time.*

A postcard from 1922 featuring the poem, "At the Foot of the Peak," by Charles Edwin Hewes who continued to run the resort through World War II and then sold it in 1945. After several owners, it was purchased by Beth Miller Harrod in 1951 and became the Rocky Ridge Music Center, a summer music camp. It was added to the National Register of Historic Places in 1994. $25+. *Courtesy of David Scarbrough, Mountain Time.*

Hewes-Kirkwood Inn, Rocky Mountain National Park, Colorado

AT THE FOOT OF THE PEAK

There's a lofty Mountain reared in the West—
    At its foot is a cabin small,
Where I dwell in that peace and quiet rest
    That comes to those who call,

To a mother of sweet and cradl'ing breast,
    Who sings when the night shades fall;
This Mountain that rears its mighty crest
    That croons with its waterfall.

©1922

Charles Edwin Hewes

Allenspark, another small mountain community, can be reached by traveling south on Highway 7 past Meeker Park. Lodges in the area included Crystal Springs, built in the early part of the 1900s and now used as a private residence; the Fawn Brook Inn, which has been operated as a restaurant for over twenty-five years; Copeland/Wild Basin Lodge; and the Ilse Trading Post as shown in this circa 1940s Sanborn postcard, $25+.

Dick Ilse built the Trading Post in the early 1930s. He was employed in nearby Longmont and spent his summers running the business. The Trading Post, now known as Allenspark Lodge, is currently operated as a bed and breakfast and owned by Bill and Juanita Martin. Dexter Press postcard, $15+.

Copeland Lake Lodge - On the South St Vrain Highway

Copeland Lake Lodge was established by the Copeland Lake Mercantile Association in 1913. It was located in the Wild Basin region near Allenspark and was one of the first lodges to have electric lights and running water in every guest room. In the 1920s the lodge was well known for its Saturday night dances. In August 1930 the *Estes Park Trail* reported the sale of Copeland Lodge to H. R. Finn who announced plans to remodel and enlarge the lodge. $25+.

Copeland Lake at Copeland Lake Lodge, Colo

Although nearby Copeland Lake was a natural lake, it was enhanced when piping was installed at the time the lodge was built. The small lake is now part of Rocky Mountain National Park. Sanborn postcard, $8-10.

After several changes in ownership, by 1948 the property had been renamed Wild Basin Lodge. This postcard was made during the ownership of Oscar and Arlene Fiene. It shows the new additions and changes made to the lodge in the 1930s. Their advertising stated that the lodge included thirty-six guest rooms, housekeeping cabins, and stables. Rex Roth purchased the lodge in 1971 and remodeled it extensively. The lodge burned in 1980 and was replaced by a new structure in 1981 that was built across the road from the original Copeland Lodge. Chester Litho, Inc. postcard, circa 1950s, $15+.

The Forks Hotel as it looked in this postcard mailed in 1907. The Forks was named for its location at the confluence of the north and south forks of the Big Thompson River. Frank Bartholf built the hotel when he learned that a new road was to be constructed through Big Thompson Canyon to Estes Park. The community was renamed Drake in 1905. Beginning in 1912 Enoch Mills managed the Forks for owner Frank Alderdyce before Mills built his own lodge, the Crags. An F. P. Clatworthy postcard, $60+.

By the 1950s, the Forks Hotel was known as the Drake General Store and Café. A post office sign is prominently displayed on the side of the building in this Dexter Press postcard. The business also advertised saddle horses and cabins. $20+.

By the 1960s, gas pumps had been added to the Drake General Store, which is now operated as the River Forks Inn. The Big Thompson flood in 1976 damaged the building, although the Forks still retains much of its original structure. New owners William and Ann Jones are restoring the hotel. Dexter Press postcard, $8-10.

Glen Haven is located seven miles north of Estes Park on Devils Gulch Road. Oren Knapp and his wife settled there in 1897. A visit to the Knapps by W. H. Shureman, a Presbyterian missionary circa 1899, chartered the future of Glen Haven. The Reverend purchased land from the Knapps to create a Presbyterian retreat where church members could buy a cabin site for fifty dollars. Shureman changed the name from Devils Canyon to Glen Haven. Shown is the Glen Haven Store that opened in 1920 and was leased to Ira Knapp. Sanborn postcard, $25+.

Glen Haven as it looked in this late 1950s view. The business district included a gift shop, café, gasoline station, livery stable, town hall, general store, and the Glen Haven Inn. The General Store is still in business after more than eighty-five years and is operated by Becky and Steve Childs. Postcard by Ray Surguine and Co., of Boulder, Colorado, $8-10.

A view of Glen Haven's Homestead Lodge, which had its beginning in 1931 when it was built by Ira Knapp who had been running the General Store. It also included cottages for rent. The building is currently operated as the Inn of Glen Haven and houses a bed and breakfast. Sanborn postcard, $30+. *Courtesy of David Scarbrough, Mountain Time.*

Part Three:
Rocky Mountain National Park

It took years of hard work for Rocky Mountain National Park to become a reality. Local naturalist Enos Mills led the effort by publishing articles, writing letters, and giving lectures to publicize the cause. Because of this, he is often called the "father" of Rocky Mountain National Park. President Woodrow Wilson signed the Rocky Mountain National Park Act designating the 229,062 acres as the country's tenth national park on January 26, 1915. It wasn't long until the Rocky Mountain Transportation Company offered daily sightseeing trips into the park. Best of all, tourists on the Circle Tour could also arrange to spend a night or two at one of the lodges in the national park.

Enos Mills was one of the speakers at the dedication of Rocky Mountain National Park on September 4, 1915, in Horseshoe Park. *Courtesy of the Enos Mills Cabin.*

Longs Peak is the highest and most visible mountain in the park with the first climbers reaching the 14,255 foot summit in 1868. It was named after Major S. H. Long, who had recorded the sighting during an expedition in 1820. The first known ascent was made by Major John Wesley Powell and William Byers, founding editor and publisher of the *Rocky Mountain News*, and their survey party. This 1920s hand-colored Clatworthy postcard is labeled "Longs Peak from Entrance to Thompson Canyon," $15+.

This postcard from the Albertype Co., of Brooklyn, New York, and published by Mrs. Enos Mills shows climbers pushing to the top of Longs Peak. The back of the postcard reads, "On the 'Home Stretch' near the top of Longs Peak. More than a thousand mountain climbers each year keep this granite trail well worn." $6-8.

"Longs Peak in the Fall," is the title of this hand-colored F. P. Clatworthy view. It also shows Longs Peak Trail. Colorado has fifty-four peaks that tower over 14,000 feet. A number of climbers set their goal to climb all of the "Fourteeners." $15+.

The Loch,
Rocky Mountain
National Park.

Rocky Mountain National Park features more than 350 miles of trails with a vast array of choices. Several of these trails are reached from the park's east side by following Bear Lake Road near the Beaver Meadow entrance west of Estes Park. One of these is the Glacier Gorge trailhead that leads to Loch Vale, a three-mile moderate hike. It is known for its spectacular beauty and grandeur and has always been popular with tourists, as shown in this early postcard by E. C. Kropp Co., of Milwaukee. $8-10.

The Bear Lake trailhead leads to several lakes, including Nymph Lake, an easy half-mile hike and one of the easiest in Rocky Mountain National Park. Postcard of Nymph Lake by Denver News Co., of Denver, Colorado. Circa 1940s, $6-8.

424—Dream Lake, Estes Park

Rocky Mountain National Park, Colorado

Dream Lake can also be reached by using the trailhead at Bear Lake. It is a moderate hike at just over one mile and is located near the base of Mt. Hallet surrounded by jagged snow covered cliffs. Sanborn postcard, $3-5.

4035 THE RANGE FROM THE HIGH DRIVE, ESTES PARK, COLORADO.
SHOWING LONG'S PEAK. ROCKY MT. NATIONAL PARK

This "The Range from High Drive" view was frequently photographed to capture the countryside's scenic vistas. Originally built as a logging road, High Drive was later used as the main road to Rocky Mountain National Park and Grand Lake. Once Trail Ridge Road was built, High Drive was closed as a through road several miles west of U.S. Highway 36 at Beaver Point. An HHT Co. postcard, $8-10.

This tree, sometimes called the Lonesome Pine Tree, or in the case of this hand-colored postcard, the Rock Tree, was located in Rocky Mountain National Park outside Estes Park near old High Drive Road. The tree grew in a small crevice surrounded by solid rock. It was about eight feet tall. It died in 1949; some speculate that hunters hastened its demise by pulling off pieces of its bark for souvenirs. It was captured by many commercial photographers through the years, including this view by F. P. Clatworthy who used the legendary tree to frame Longs Peak. $15+.

Early view of a camping tent on the shore of Bear Lake located at the end of Bear Lake Road in Rocky Mountain National Park. It may have been one of the tents rented to tourists as part of an early enterprise called Bear Lake Camp. By 1920 Frank Byerly was the owner of several primitive buildings in the area, which, at the time, could only be reached by a primitive road. A W. T. Parke postcard, $20+.

BEAR LAKE. ESTES PARK

A new road to Bear Lake was built in the early 1920s that allowed easier access to Byerly's Bear Lake Lodge, which by then included a new one-story building called the Upper Lodge. It held the dining room and some guest facilities. Later, Lower Lodge, a two-story log building, was built as shown, circa late 1920s or early 1930s. The first floor included a small store, soda fountain, and office. The second floor was used for dances and a lounge. $15+. *Courtesy of the Colorado Collection/Estes Park Public Library.*

A view of the dining room in Upper Lodge – a large fireplace dominates the room. Also shown is a matchbook cover from the same period listing activities including saddle livery, pack trips, swimming, hiking, climbing, and fries and picnics. Sometime after Byerly married Edna Bishop, she and her two sons, James and Charles, began managing the resort. By 1940 there were thirty-four rooms that could be used to house sixty-five guests. Operating at the highest elevation of any lodge in the park, the season didn't get underway until mid June because of the cold. Circa late 1930s or early 1940s. Sanborn postcard, $15+; matchbook, $10.

Another Sanborn view shows the cocktail lounge at Bear Lake's Lower Lodge. Edna Bishop died in 1956 and her family continued to operate the lodge until 1958 when the lease with the park ended. Upper Lodge was moved from the grounds and is being used at Elk Meadow Lodge & RV Resort near Estes Park. Other buildings were torn down so the land could be returned to its natural state. $15. *Courtesy of David Scarbrough, Mountain Time.*

A Bear Lake Lodge promotional brochure. Circa 1950s, $60+.

Less accessible was Fern Lodge on Fern Lake, which could only be reached by trail. It was built in 1911 by Dr. William Workman. Besides the lodge, tent and log cabins were eventually added. Several different owners ran the lodge until 1959 when the park lease was not renewed. Park workers burned the lodge in 1976 because of recurring vandalism. Sanborn postcard, $30+. *Courtesy of David Scarbrough, Mountain Time.*

FOREST INN AT THE POOL

ESTES PARK, COLO.

A brochure for the Forest Inn at the Pool, located west of Estes Park along Fern Lake Trail. Frank and Fannie Tecker bought the remote property in 1917 and a resort began to take shape. In 1919 a fire destroyed most of what they had built, but in 1929, a new lodge was opened. Until then, the Teckers made do with tents and a few cabins that were accessed by foot or horseback. By the 1930s the last cabins had been built. After the 1952 season, Tecker sold the property to the park and the buildings were demolished in 1959. $40+. *From the Scarbrough collection.*

THE BRINWOOD, ESTES PARK

The Brinwood Hotel was owned by Sally and Charles Reed who began building the hotel around 1910 in Moraine Park. The original building was two stories tall and included an office, lobby, kitchen, and dining room on the first floor, and guest rooms on the second floor. $30+. *Courtesy of the Colorado Collection/Estes Park Public Library.*

Eventually the Reeds had twenty-nine buildings on the property, housing up to one hundred guests. The Depression brought hard times and the Brinwood was purchased by the Park Service in 1932. The owners received a twenty-year operating permit and continued to run the hotel for nearly fifteen more years. Sanborn postcard, $10+.

417—The Brinwood Hotel, Estes Park, Colorado

In Rocky Mountain National Park

8A149-N

ROCKY MOUNTAIN NATIONAL PARK, COLORADO.

The Brinwood and the remaining years of its lease were sold in 1947 to the Brinwood Ranch-Hotel Corporation, which continued in business until 1958. The buildings were demolished in 1960. The pictured business card reads, "Where the Road Ends and the Trails Begin." Sanborn postcard, $8-10; business card, $8.

Stead's Hotel, Moraine Park, Colo.

What became the Stead's Hotel was built on land homesteaded by Abner Sprague in the 1870s and was later known as Moraine Park, located about five miles southwest of Estes Park. With additions, the hotel reached three stories. The Sprague family continued to run the hotel until 1902 when they added new partners, Mr. and Mrs. James Stead from Chicago. The new partners soon bought the business and in 1904 the name was changed to Stead's Ranch. A W. T. Parke postcard, $20+.

As this view from the 1920s shows, the Stead's Ranch continued to grow. In addition to lodge buildings and employee housing, there were over twenty cottages of various sizes at the time this postcard was mailed. James Stead died in 1931. His wife Dora joined with relatives to run the ranch until her death in 1936. The family continued to carry on its operation. A Clatworthy hand-colored postcard, $15+.

A swimming pool was added to Stead's after it was sold to Mr. and Mrs. Edgar Stopher in 1950. Other improvements included an extension of the dance hall to be used for square dancing. The ranch was sold to the national park in 1962 and the buildings were removed. Flatirons Post Card Co., of Boulder, Colorado, $6-8.

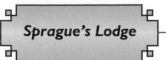

Glacier Basin, Rocky Mountain National Park.

In 1914, ten years after Abner and Alberta Sprague sold their lodge to James Stead, they began converting their summer home to accommodate tourists. It was located off Bear Lake Road in Glacier Basin. In those early years, the property was referred to as Glacier Basin Lodge. $30+. *Courtesy of David Scarbrough, Mountain Time*.

465 - Spragues Lodge and Snow Capped Range in Glacier Basin, Rocky Mountain National Park, Colorado

This later view shows the establishment after the lodge was completed. It included a dining room, lounge, kitchen, bathroom, laundry, and seventeen guest rooms. The lodge was sold to the Park Service in 1932 and Abner Sprague was granted a lease to continue operating the lodge for twenty years. $25+.

Sprague's Lodge as it looked at the end of its tenure under Edgar Stopher's ownership. He ended his lease early and it closed in 1957. Most of the buildings were demolished by 1960. Entertainment included fishing, hiking, horseback riding, and square dancing. The matchbook cover advertises both Sprague's and Stead's when the Stophers owned both properties. Sanborn postcard, $10-12; matchbook, $10.

Moraine Lodge, Moraine, Colo.

Moraine Lodge was founded by Imogene MacPherson and her husband William in Moraine Park. The first building was built in 1905 and the lodge welcomed its first guests in 1910. Additional facilities were added that included cabins, a stable, main lodge, and dining room. Although Mr. MacPherson passed away in 1919, his wife continued to operate the lodge. $30+. *Courtesy of the Colorado Collection/Estes Park Public Library*.

Imogene MacPherson died in 1928 at the age of eighty-four. The lodge continued to operate until the end of the 1931 season. The property became part of the national park in 1932. Although the other lodge buildings were demolished, the assembly hall, which was built in 1923, was saved and has been used as the Moraine Park Museum since 1937 and is operated by the Park Service. Pictured is a hand-colored F. P. Clatworthy postcard showing the assembly hall on right. Circa 1920s, $15+.

This William Allen White cabin belonged to the famous editor of the *Emporia Gazette*. White purchased the cabin in 1912 and spent many summers here with his family. The small-town Kansas editor was nationally known for his editorials and his poignant piece written after his teenage daughter died in a horse-riding accident. The cabin is located above Moraine Park and the view, as shown, is spectacular. In 1972 the family sold the cabin to the Park Service; it's currently used for its Artist in Residence program.

MORAINE PARK, ESTES PARK, COLO.

Moraine Park

Early view of Moraine Park — the way it used to look when a small summer community occupied the area southwest of Estes Park. Included were Stead's Lodge, a store-post office, many private cabins, and Moraine Lodge and Brinwood Lodge, which were nearby. For more information on lodges in the park, refer to *Those Castles of Wood* by Henry F. Pedersen, Jr. A W. T. Parke postcard, $10-12.

In 1917 Orville W. Bechtel established a store on land he homesteaded eight miles west of Estes Park to sell his photographs, lunches, and refreshments. The business was sold in the late 1920s to the Gustave Schubert family. A fifty-foot-tall observation tower was built on the property circa 1933, as shown in this Sanborn postcard. $30+.

The Schubert family expanded the Deer Ridge property and a replacement tower was built atop a new addition that included a dining room. The Schuberts provided food, rental cabins, souvenirs, Indian wares, and rental horses. After the deaths of the elder Schuberts, their children continued to run the business. Postcard by J. A. Ossen Company, of Denver, Colorado, $15+.

Deer Ridge Chalet as it looked in its last years in the 1950s. The back of this postcard states the chalet was the largest souvenir gift shop in the U.S.A. Also shown is a Deer Ridge Chalet souvenir pencil. The Park Service had been eager to purchase the chalet for many years and by 1960 had acquired all of the Deer Ridge buildings, many of which were relocated. Flatiron Postcard Co., $10-12; pencil, $15.

91034. Horseshoe Inn, Estes Park, Colorado.
ROCKY MOUNTAIN NATIONAL PARK.

Willard and Grace Ashton purchased property in Horseshoe Park in 1905 while on a summer trip to Estes Park. They decided to build a tourist facility on the acreage in 1908 and the Horseshoe Inn opened in 1909. It was located along Fall River Road. An HHT Co. postcard, $20+.

15379. Horseshoe Inn, Estes Park, Colorado
Rocky Mountain National Park

7802
HORSE SHOE FALLS
ESTES PARK, COLO.

Horseshoe Inn provided horses to its guests with a livery stable shared with Fall River Lodge. The inn was sold to Harry Bradley and Claude Patrick in 1915. In 1917 a four-story addition to the inn was built. Because of hard times from the Depression, the inn was sold to the Park Service in 1931, the first year the Park Service began acquiring such properties, and the inn was burned that fall. An HHT Co. postcard postmarked 1931, $10-12.

Horseshoe Falls near Fall River Road. The falls extend for nearly a mile on the Roaring River, which brings the snowy waters of the Mummy Range down to Horseshoe Park. An HHT Co. postcard, $3-5.

Cascade Lodge

The Cascade Lodge was thought to be built by W. S. Magers and a partner in Horseshoe Park. Opened in 1925, it included a lodge building that housed a lobby, dining room, and twenty guest rooms with baths. Several cabins were included on the property. The lodge was purchased by Anna May Derby in the late 1920s. Her ownership was cut short on June 12, 1935, when the lodge caught fire and burned. The lodge was not rebuilt although the remaining cottages, and others added to the property, continue to be rented. The L. V. Davis family has maintained ownership of the Cascade Cottages since 1941. It is the only remaining privately owned lodging facility within the park. Sanborn postcard, $30+. *Courtesy of David Scarbrough, Mountain Time.*

The interior of Cascade Lodge as it looked when it opened in 1925 furnished with rustic hickory furniture. This postcard was mailed in 1925 — the first summer that classes were held there by the Rocky Mountain Biological Station of Denver University. Students could receive college credit in botany and zoology. The back of the postcard includes this message from one of the students, "I have been here for a month taking credits toward a minor in botany. This lodge has a beautifully rustic living room." $25+. *Courtesy of David Scarbrough, Mountain Time.*

Fall River Lodge was built by Dan and Minnie March in 1915. It was located in the western end of Horseshoe Park, which served as the site for the dedication of Rocky Mountain National Park later in the year. An HHT Co. postcard, $20+.

FALL RIVER
Lodge and Ranch
Estes Park, Colorado

Located in the Rocky Mountain National Park

"The Playground of America"

This Fall River Lodge brochure described guest activities that included "horseback riding, hiking, dancing in the new pavilion, tennis, fishing, autoing, nature talks, and Kodaking." In 1935, ten years after Dan March died, Minnie married Sam Service, who had run the general store in Estes for many years. Circa 1930s, $15+.

The main lodge building eventually grew to three stories that included rooms for thirty-five guests with private baths. Other guests could be housed in nearby cabins. In 1941 Russell McKelvey and his wife Florence purchased Fall River Lodge and continued its operation until it was sold to the National Park Service in 1955. The lodge was closed in 1959 and the buildings were demolished. Sanborn postcard, $3-5.

15649. Gateway, Fall River Entrance, Rocky Mountain National Park

This HHT Co. postcard shows the early Estes Park entrance to Rocky Mountain National Park that was completed in 1920 at Horseshoe Park. Because of the increase in automobile traffic, speeds were limited to twelve miles per hour. By the start of the 1922 season, the *Estes Park Trail* was reporting visitation had surpassed all other national parks in the country and promised to break previous attendance records for the coming season. The park entrance was eventually moved to the east where the Fall River entrance stands today. $35+. *Courtesy David Scarbrough, Mountain Time.*

Construction of Fall River Road began in 1913 to link Estes Park and Grand Lake, with Roe Emery directing its eventual completion in 1920 after several contracting companies walked off the job. His involvement in the road's construction was recalled during an interview published in the *Rocky Mountain News* on October 30, 1949. Although the new state-built road was a success, Emery noted that his Circle Tour drivers had to back up three or four times to negotiate its sharp curves and narrow width as they traversed the most difficult of the twenty-three switchbacks. Brake repairs were necessary after every trip. Hand-colored postcard by F. P. Clatworthy, circa 1920s, $15+.

451   SNOW CAÑON AT THE SUMMIT OF THE FALL RIVER ROAD.

ESTES PARK—GRAND LAKE ROAD, ROCKY MOUNTAIN NATIONAL PARK, COLO.   116962

In addition to the perils of the narrow Fall River Road, snow removal was also a challenge for the new passageway. At first crews opened the road with shovels each spring, but by the time this postcard was issued, "a large gang of men and a steam shovel begin a thirty-day campaign to open up Fall River Road for travel." In 1929 the state allowed the federal government to take over the roads in the park. By then, the Park Service had already experienced difficulties with the narrow, winding Fall River Road and was making plans to build another more suitable road for mountain travel at the urging of transportation pioneer Roe Emery. Sanborn postcard, $3-5.

436   SHELTER HOUSE AT SUMMIT OF THE FALL RIVER ROAD

ALT. 11,797 FEET, GRAND LAKE—ESTES PARK ROAD, COLORADO   113312

A shelter cabin was built at the summit of Fall River Pass in 1920 to be used during sudden snowstorms and other emergencies. The cabin was built of stone and was equipped with a fireplace and firewood. It provided shelter for snowbound auto parties until relief could be sent. Call stations were also installed along the route, following installation of telephone lines, so tourists could call for help in an emergency. Sanborn postcard, $3-5.

C.406   LAKE HAIYAHA AND LONG'S PEAK,

ROCKY MOUNTAIN NATIONAL PARK, COLO.   3A-H439

CRYSTAL LAKE, ESTES PARK, COLO.   11710

There are 450 miles of streams and 150 lakes within Rocky Mountain National Park, including Lake Haiyaha, which has attracted many visitors since the early days. This Sanborn postcard describes Lake Haiyaha as typical of the many small alpine lakes in the vicinity of Bear Lake and Longs Peak. The card indicates Lake Haiyaha means "rock bound in the Indian tongue." $10-12.

Near Mt. Ypsilon is beautiful Crystal Lake. This early postcard offered visitors a tantalizing view of this hard to reach place. The lake can be found by following the Lawn Lake Trail, passing by Lawn Lake, and completing a hike that is nearly eight miles long in one direction. Postcard published by Acmegraph Co., of Chicago, Illinois, $10-12.

Construction began on the new Trail Ridge Road circa 1930 with separate crews working on the Estes and Grand Lake sides of the project. The road opened in 1932. This Sanborn postcard pictures the loops on the wider Trail Ridge Road above Hidden Valley and Horseshoe Park, $3-5.

405 MT. YPSILON, ALTITUDE 13,507 FEET, FROM THE SWITCHBACKS ON THE TRAIL RIDGE ROAD, ESTES PARK

GRAND LAKE HIGHWAY, ROCKY MT. NATIONAL PARK, COLO.

Souvenir windshield stickers were first issued to Rocky Mountain visitors in 1922. In creating the keepsakes, each national park was given its own distinctive color and an animal was depicted typical of the region. The sticker for RMNP was green and showed a bighorn sheep. It was not until 1939 that an entry free of $1 per car was charged as shown on this 1941 permit. Souvenir sticker, $35+; permit, $10+.

This Sanborn view shows Mt. Ypsilon as well as the switchback on Trail Ridge Road. The road traveled to the top of Fall River Pass and up the east side of the Continental Divide before making its way down the western slope. Circa 1930s, $3-5.

This Sanborn postcard shows the big rock ledges on Trail Ridge Road. The ledges are reached at an altitude of about 12,000 feet. The rock wall along the highway was constructed by the Civilian Conservation Corps whose members were housed near Estes Park and Grand Lake to work on park projects beginning in 1933. The Estes Park camps were located in Horseshoe and Hallowell parks. $3-5.

451—Tundra Curves at Altitude of 12,000 Feet on the Trail Ridge Road,

Rocky Mountain National Park, Colorado
7A70-N

Continuing the climb along the road, this Sanborn postcard describes the journey to its highest point. "The Tundra Curves take the traveler up the last great rise on the Trail Ridge Road to reach the highest point on this lofty trip at 12,183 ft. altitude." $3-5.

C.C.C. Camp
N.P.7.
Grand Lake
Colo.

The C.C.C. (Civilian Conservation Corps) Camp on the western side of Rocky Mountain National Park was located at Phantom Valley. The tent camp is shown on this postcard, which was mailed in 1939. Most of the money the young men earned was sent to their families. They worked on trails, constructed buildings, and carried out other duties to help the park rangers. $25+.

This view marks the highest point on Trail Ridge Road. It remains the highest paved continuous road in the U.S. Postcard by Ray Surguine News Agency, of Boulder, Colorado, $3-5.

Shown is Milner Pass and Poudre Lakes at the Continental Divide on Trail Ridge Road. The road skirts the lakes, which feed their water to the Atlantic while the water to the west of this point flows to the Pacific. Sanborn postcard, $3-5.

The Trail Ridge Store and Museum, elevation 11,797 feet, was opened by Roe Emery of the Rocky Mountain Parks Transportation Co. in 1937. Indian jewelry, rugs and blankets, pottery and baskets, and food were sold. Emery sold the business to brothers Ted and I. B. James in 1953 and they operated the facility until the end of the 1982 season. It was then sold to Forever Resorts. The Alpine Visitor Center located next to the store opened in 1965 in honor of the park's 50th anniversary as part of the Mission 66 improvement program. Sanborn postcard, $3-5.

The James family members were also park concessionaires for the Hidden Valley Ski Area near Estes Park from 1955 to 1977. Skiing at Hidden Valley was popular on an informal basis even before the James era. In 1954 the Park Service built a warming house and a 400-car parking lot. As part of its Mission 66 program, the government also built a ski lodge-cafeteria. During Ted James' operation, ski rental facilities, lifts, and new ski trails were developed. In 1978 the National Park Service took control of the ski area after James suffered financial difficulties. Hidden Valley Lodge postcard by Flatiron Post Card Co., $20+; souvenir ski patch, $20+.

The Estes Valley Recreation and Park District operated the ski area from 1978 until it closed in 1992. The Park Service had subsidized the business for several years because of a seventy-five percent decline in skiers during its last ten years of operation. The buildings and the parking lot were removed. In 2004 the park opened a new facility in Hidden Valley that included restrooms, a warming hut, ranger office, parking, and picnic area. Visitors were encouraged to return to Hidden Valley for snowshoeing and back country skiing in the winter, and hiking and picnicking in the summer. Shown is a brochure from 1991, one of the last years of operation for the Hidden Valley Ski Area. It included four trails serviced by three lifts. *Courtesy of the Lula W. Dorsey Museum.*

As Trail Ridge Road continues toward Grand Lake, visitors experience the Never Summer Range that towers over the Kawuneeche Valley. Located there is the Grand Ditch, one of the oldest transmountain diversion projects in the state that channels water to northern Colorado. The fourteen-mile long project was built over a thirty-year period beginning in 1894 and continues to be owned and operated by the Water Supply and Storage Company of Fort Collins, Colorado. It was placed on the National Register of Historic Places in 1976. Sanborn postcard, $3-5.

In 1956 the National Park Service announced its ambitious ten-year Mission 66 program to enhance visitor enjoyment and protect unimpaired park lands. During this time most of the lodges and ranches surrounding Rocky Mountain National Park were purchased and the land was incorporated into the park. New structures were also to be added in time for the park's 50th anniversary, including a new contemporary Beaver Meadows Visitor Center designed by Taliesin Associated Architects, who had been affiliated with Frank Lloyd Wright. Visitors began using the center in 1967, and in 2001 it was selected as a National Landmark for its "organic architecture." Postcard by Kadlecek Studios, of Greeley, Colorado, $20+. *Courtesy of the Estes Park Museum.*

In 1907 Robert "Squeaky Bob" Wheeler filed a homestead claim for 160 acres twelve miles north of Grand Lake. It was the only stopping place between Horseshoe Inn in Estes Park and Grand Lake. When Wheeler decided to turn the homestead into a resort, he added several tent houses and called it "Hotel De Hardscrabble." He had a high squeaky voice, which guaranteed his nickname, and could always be found with his dog Jack, as shown. Wheeler sold his establishment in 1926-27 to Lester Scott before moving to Denver where he died in 1946. Scott built a new lodge and cabins and changed the name to Phantom Valley Ranch. *Courtesy of Jane Kemp.*

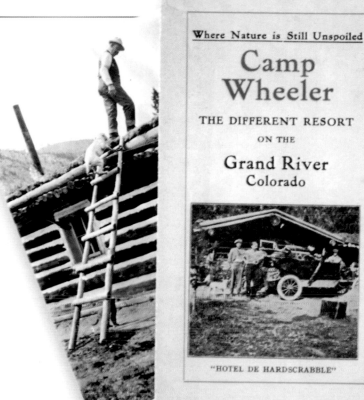

Where Nature is Still Unspoiled

Camp Wheeler

THE DIFFERENT RESORT

ON THE

Grand River
Colorado

"HOTEL DE HARDSCRABBLE"

In 1941 Phantom Valley Ranch was sold to Irwin Beattie. He was still advertising the ranch in 1958. It became a part of the national park in 1960. This Sanborn postcard shows guests gathered in front of the main lodge, which was used as a dining room and lounge. Circa 1940s, $20+.

This Sanborn postcard shows the interior of the Phantom Valley Ranch Lodge. Circa 1940s, $30+.

Holzwarth Trout Lodge was opened ten miles north of Grand Lake by Sophia and John Holzwarth on land they had homesteaded since 1917. With Fall River Road opening in 1920, the Holzwarths found it more profitable to house and feed tourists in their home than continue their ranching operation. This advertisement was carried in the 1924 edition of the *Highway Map Service*.

HOLZWARTH TROUT LODGE

Ten Miles North of Grand Lake on Fall River Road.

Three Miles of Trout Stream on Our Property

Camps—Saddle Horses
Completely Furnished Cottages
Excellent Home Cooked Meals

Grand Lake, Colorado

Holzwarth's Never Summer Ranch circa 1950s. By 1973 Johnnie was no longer able to manage the business, but wanted the property to be preserved as open space, which was successfully arranged. It has been owned by the national park since 1974. The Never Summer Ranch buildings were torn down while the earlier Holzwarth property has been preserved as a history museum. Rocky Mt. View Co. postcard, $15+.

By the 1930s the Holzwarths had developed nicer guest ranch facilities on property the family owned near Trail Ridge Road. The Holzwarth ranch included a "rustic lodge, with suites and private baths," according to the pictured brochure issued by son Johnnie Holzwarth who was then in charge of operating the business. This Christmas card shows the lodge circa late 1950s. Brochure, $10; card, $15+.

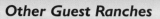

KAWUNEECHE RANCH   Grand Lake, Colorado

Kawuneeche Ranch was located seven miles north of Grand Lake and became a guest ranch in the 1930s. In 1940 owner A. N. House ran the ranch, which included "housekeeping cabins, good fishing, and saddle horses." The property was purchased by the Park Service in 1967. $20+. *Courtesy of David Scarbrough, Mountain Time.*

ONAHU RANCH
GRAND LAKE, COLO.

Green Mountain Ranch was founded by Carl and Ada Nelson near Onahu Creek in 1934. It included a house and several cabins and was located near Trail Ridge Road five miles north of Grand Lake. The ranch offered "riding, fishing, and excellent food." It was purchased by the Park Service in 1972. Postcard by Steamboat Pilot, of Steamboat Springs, Colorado, $8-10.

Onahu Ranch was located in the national park five miles north of Grand Lake near Onahu Creek. In 1940, ads listed the owner as Myrle Hall with operations that included a lodge, rental cabins, saddle horses, and pack trips. Others operated the facility mostly as a dude ranch until the 1960s when it was purchased by the National Park Service. Some of its buildings were retained and used for employee housing. $20+.

One of Rocky Mountain National Park's most unusual sites is the Grand Lake Cemetery, founded in 1875 and located west of the Kawuneeche Visitor Center. At the town's request, a permanent cemetery use permit was issued by the federal government in 1997. The town administers the cemetery while the Grand Lake Women's Club keeps the property tidy as it has done since the club's founding in 1912. The pictured gravestone was placed in remembrance of sisters Annie and Kitty Harbison who each homesteaded 160 acres in 1896. They lived on their property until their deaths in 1938. The land is now part of the national park.

Some gravesites in the Grand Lake Cemetery are enclosed with traditional wood or iron fences while others are outlined with rocks. Relatives decorate graves with items that are reminders of their loved ones using skis, handmade wooden grave markers, or mementos of the person's life. The pictured grave of pioneer plumber Gustave Anton Spitzmiller features a large hand-made pipe wrench to pay tribute to his profession.

ADAMS FALLS - GRAND LAKE COLO - G 961

Adams Falls, formerly called Ousel Falls, is located on Grand Lake's East Inlet. In 1907, area residents renamed it in honor of Jay E. Adams. The Adams family was among the first to build a summer home on the shores of Grand Lake circa 1889. The hike is less than a mile for the round trip and is the most popular outing for families and others looking for a short but scenic journey. Postcard by Great Western Post Card Co., of Denver, Colorado, $10-12.

A Sanborn postcard of the Shadow Mountain Fire Lookout Tower near Grand Lake. It was placed on the National Register of Historic Places in 1978. The rock building was built in the 1930s and measures thirteen square feet and three stories high. The ranger occupied the third floor where a telephone and radio kept him in contact with authorities. In a dry season, the ranger was required to check-in once each hour. It is the only fire lookout tower remaining in the park and hikers can reach the site by using the trailhead on the east side of Shadow Mountain Lake, just south of Grand Lake. It is a strenuous hike with a round trip distance of 9.4 miles. The building was restored in 1992. $15+.

Shadow Mountain Lake and Lake Granby are part of the Shadow Mountain National Recreation Area established in 1952. Also included are the federal lands around the lakes. The lakes were made as part of the Colorado-Big Thompson water project built by the Bureau of Reclamation and are linked by a channel to Grand Lake. Postcard of Grand Lake and Shadow Mountain Lake by Flatiron, of Boulder, Colorado, $3-5.

Granby Dam and Reservoir, located between Granby and Grand lakes, is pictured on a postcard by Curteich Color. A pumping plant on Lake Granby sends water through the Alva B. Adams Tunnel and under the Continental Divide to the east slope to be used for irrigation. Both residents and tourists have benefited from the project as more fishing, boating, and camping opportunities have been provided because of this government project. $3-5.

Part Four:

Grand Lake

The beautiful setting of Grand Lake with Mt. Craig in the background is among the most scenic sites along the Circle Tour. It is the largest natural body of water in Colorado. Although the Ute Indians camped in the Grand Lake area for hundreds of years, Judge Joseph L. Wescott was its first permanent settler. He was also the first to accommodate tourists. The Civil War veteran came to Grand Lake in 1867 and established his homestead on the west shore of the lake. Westcott persevered through financial hardships and many harsh winters and remained a Grand Lake resident until his death in 1914. He offered hospitality to hunters and fishermen in his early years and made a better life for himself in his later years by dividing his homestead into lots that he sold to visitors for summer cabins. In 1877 he became Grand Lake's first postmaster.

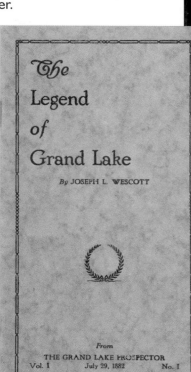

The
Legend
of
Grand Lake

By JOSEPH L. WESCOTT

From
THE GRAND LAKE PROSPECTOR
Vol. 1   July 29, 1882   No. 1

Shown is a booklet containing "The Legend of Grand Lake," a poem by Joseph L. Wescott from the *Grand Lake Prospector*, July 29, 1882, and reprinted in 1926 by Fred H. Quincy, of Salina, Kansas. The poem begins, "White man, pause and gaze around/For we tread now on haunted ground! So said a chief to me one day/As along the shore we wound our way." Wescott's poem describes a tale told by the Ute Indians that occurred while they were camping near Grand Lake. A fierce storm descended upon the camp and allowed rival tribes to attack the Utes. To save the women and children from their enemies, they were placed on rafts and pushed out into the water. After the stormy battle, the Ute warriors realized the rafts had overturned and all the women and children had drowned. To this day, many consider the lake to be haunted with spirits rising from the mist as illustrated by this Sanborn postcard, $3-5; booklet, $10+.

Grand Lake Village

After a period of economic depression when mining in the area collapsed after the boom years of 1879 to 1883, Grand Lake eventually found its niche by expanding its tourist opportunities. Hotels, cabins, and summer homes provided places for visitors to stay and the lake and surrounding countryside provided an abundance of recreation. Fishing, boating, and hiking became popular for tourists of all ages and, with the addition of snowmobiling, remain so today. With the opening of Rocky Mountain National Park in 1915, Grand Lake became the town nearest the western entrance to the park and was blessed to receive a steady stream of tourists who visited Grand Lake each summer.

This early view shows the town of Grand Lake with the lake in the background. Postcard published by Out West Photo, of Boulder, Colorado, $15+.

"Giant Post Card" of Grand Lake, featuring a sailboat and Mt. Craig (Baldy) in the background along with a tourist brochure circa mid-1930s. The brochure was issued by the Grand Lake Commercial Association and included many of the businesses in the area: the Corner Cupboard and Tavern, Holzwarth's Dude Ranch, Kauffman House, Pine Cone Inn, Zick's Hotel and Cottages, Brownhurst Cottages, Cross Roads Cottage Camp, Daven Haven Cottage Camp, Iron Kettle Inn, Nair's Red and White Store, Thompson's Grocery, Matilda G. Humphrey's Store, Grand Lake Garage, the Rustic Stables, and Fred. E. Maker Insurance and Real Estate. Postcard, $10; brochure, $15+.

Longtime Grand Lake resident H. A. (Harry) Bunte operated the Rustic Stables on Grand Avenue for many years. By 1940 Bunte's businesses included a new Rustic Court with "extra clean, completely modern cabins." He also operated a service station and an auto repair garage on the site. By the 1960s the units were known as the Bunk'n Bronco Cabins owned by Barbara and Rocky Garber. Under new ownership in the early 1980s, an explosion during renovations made it necessary to demolish the stable buildings. A bowling alley was later built on the site. This postcard mailed in 1942 pictures the Rustic Cabin Court, Stables and Garage. The author writes, "We're in the cabin I've marked 'x'. We've driven all around, viewed the lake, shopped the stores, eaten the food and are having a grand time." $15+.

"View of the street at Grand Lake, Colo." The large building on the left was originally home of the Grand Lake Mercantile Store opened in 1906 by Harry Harbison, who had also served as postmaster. Earlier postcards showed the building with a large "Post Office" sign on its roof and a sign identifying the business as "The Red and White Store." In 1924 it was the "Pine Tree Trading Post/ Fred Maker's Place/Post Office." This postcard dates from a few years later and pictures the historic building, which is still standing today. Sanborn postcard, $20+.

Zick family members had a business presence in Grand Lake for more than seventy-five years. The first of the family businesses was opened by Mr. and Mrs. John Zick in 1918: they began a grocery store in the building that formerly housed the county courthouse when Grand Lake was the county seat from 1881-1888. It grew to include a meat market, restaurant, and hotel. Sanborn postcard mailed in 1929, $50+.

GRAND LAKE

Stop at

ZICK'S

Up-to-Date

HOTEL
GROCERY - MARKET
RESTAURANT

Rooms and Cottages

GRAND LAKE   COLORADO

This Zick's brochure describes the various Zick enterprises. The grocery store was known for its fresh meats, dairy, and produce, while the restaurant offered "good home-cooked meals." In addition to the hotel, cottages were available. Pictured is the Daisy Cottage, one of the rental units located behind the hotel-store. Circa 1940s, $15+.

Son Ray Zick began work in the grocery store in 1948. The pictured menu lists hotcakes and coffee for twenty cents and dinners for sixty-five cents. Eventually Ray and wife Ruth took over the business and operated the grocery store, at left, until their retirement circa 1979. Flatiron Postcard Co., $6-8; menu, $10+.

MENU

ZICK'S

Established 1918

GRAND LAKE, COLO.

Early Grand Lake businessman James Cairns built the first building after the town site was surveyed and platted in 1881. His general merchandise store operated in this building until 1908, when he built his second store. He continued to operate the business until he sold it to Matilda G. Humphrey in 1924. This view, titled "Sports at Grand Lake, Colo.," pictures the Cairns Store at right. Postcard from Out West Photo, of Boulder, Colorado. Circa 1912, $45+. *Courtesy of David Scarbrough, Mountain Time.*

Matilda Humphrey eventually enlarged the Cairns building and by 1940 advertised products and services that included drugs, gifts, photo shop, beauty parlor, barbershop, soda fountain, and room rentals above the business. Mrs. Humphrey's brother Leonard Zick worked at the store for many years and was Grand Lake's first elected mayor after the town was incorporated in 1944. Circa early 1940s, $30+.

Jeanette Akolt took over the business in the early 1970s after her mother's death. After Akolt's retirement in the late 1990s, the building was leased to others. Flatiron Postcard, $6-8.

Grand Lake Village, Colorado

Grand Lake street scene showing Thompson's Grocery on the right front. Ads of the era listed fresh vegetables, meats, and cabins. Sanborn postcard, circa 1930s, $20+.

Bill (W.T.) and Cora Lehman were active in the Grand Lake business community for many years. In the early 1920s, they ran Lehman's Hotel. By the 1930s, the couple operated Bill's Place Café on Grand Avenue. It is pictured on the right in this Sanborn postcard. On the left is the sign for the Iron Kettle Inn owned by Ray and Edna Ruske. It opened as a restaurant in the 1930s, but was later transformed into the Cottage Grocery. Two rental cabins behind the store were also part of the business. The grocery was destroyed in 1943 as a result of the Pine Cone Inn fire. $15+.

By the 1950s Cora Lehman had opened a smaller restaurant one block south of Grand Avenue. The two-story building included rooms Cora rented to college girls who worked in the village during the summer. $10+.

Community House. Grand Lake, Colorado.

The Grand Lake Community House was built in 1922 with donated money and labor. Through the years it has been used for public functions, minstrel shows, holiday celebrations, social affairs, club meetings, community center, and live theater. It also served as a summer movie theater from 1936 through the early 1980s. Postcard by Geo. T. Huling, of Denver, Colorado. $15+.

The Grand Lake School was held in a variety of temporary spaces until the first one-room school was built in 1910. Shown is a larger school that was constructed in 1935. It housed grades one through eight and included two large classrooms with four grades in each room. The basement was later made into additional classrooms. It was used until 1958 when the school was consolidated into a larger district in East Grand County. This building is now used as a church. Students who wanted additional education in the early years went to live with relatives who had a high school nearby if possible. Other families spent the winters in other locations and called Grand Lake home only in the summers. Sanborn postcard, $15+.

St. Anne's Catholic Church was completed in 1958. The new parish had been established in 1944. Before the church was built, mass had been held in a building first used for worship in 1918. The new church could seat 270 people. The statue of St. Anne above the main entrance was made of cast stone by carvers from Tyrol, Austria. They also made the eleven foot hand-carved wooden crucifix above the main alter. Monsignor Thomas Barry was instrumental in raising money to build the church. Sanborn postcard, $3-5.

The Little Church in the Pines was organized as the Grand Lake Community Presbyterian Church in 1937. Fund-raising events were held to keep the church going and eventually the congregation built a building on land donated by Mrs. Mary Cairns and her daughter Patience. The church was built and dedicated in 1942. Postcard by Colorado Specta-Vues, of Arapaho Valley Ranch, Granby, Colorado, $3-5.

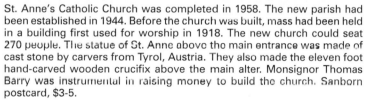

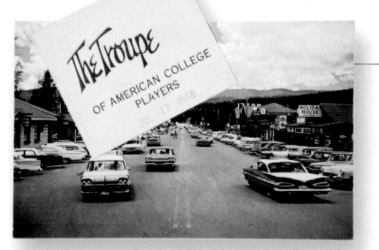

This winter view of Grand Lake Village no longer represents a typical Grand Lake winter scene. Instead, there would be foot, snowmobile, and auto traffic filling the main street of the village. Grand Lake is now known as the "Snowmobile Capital of Colorado." There are 180 miles of snowmobile trails around Grand Lake, including a connecting trail to those in the national park. Approximately 125 miles of these trails are groomed nightly by the volunteer Grand Lake Trail Groomers Association. The snowmobilers who come to visit have helped to make Grand Lake a winter resort as well as a summer paradise. Postcard by Colorado Specta-Vues, of Granby, Colorado. Circa 1970s, $3-5.

Live theater came to Grand Lake in 1967 when David Thompson brought his Troupe of American College Players to town with support from the Grand Lake Women's Club. The plays were performed at the Pine Cone Inn. After the original theater was demolished, performances were held in a variety of locations, including the town's Community Building. Following the Troupe's departure, live theater continued in Grand Lake with summer productions by the Players, and most recently, the Rocky Mountain Repertory Theatre. Shown is the original home of the Troupe, the Pine Cone Inn, on the left. A ticket stub from July 17, 1969, is also shown. Postcard by Colorado Spectra-Vues, of Granby, Colorado, $3-5. *Ticket courtesy of Bob Scott.*

Hotels/Cabins

The earliest Grand Lake hotels had their beginnings in the late 1870s and early 1880s. They included the Grand Lake House constructed in 1878; the Grand Central Hotel, also known as the Nickerson House, built in 1880; Fairview House and the Garrison House, both built in 1881; the Kauffman House in 1892; the Rustic Hotel circa 1900; and the Bellevue in 1902. Only the Kauffman House remains today, but it was due to these hoteliers' early vision that paved the way for Grand Lake's future prosperity.

The Rustic Hotel had its beginning in 1889 when Chris and Josie Young began building a hotel on land given to them by Chris' mother Mary Jane Young in 1887. She had moved to Grand Lake in 1878 and filed a homestead claim that included land on the west side of Grand Lake, where she oversaw construction of her Fairview House Hotel. It was near this hotel's ice house on July 4, 1883 that an infamous massacre occurred, eventually costing six lives, following an argument by rival politicians over control of the county commissioners. The nearby Rustic Hotel became a work in progress as Chris and Josie added to the enterprise as money permitted. Three children were born to the couple including a son, Jake. Chris died in 1905. This Rustic Hotel advertisement is postmarked 1916 after Josie had married H. C. Langley in 1906. The postcard lists Mrs. Josie Langley as the proprietor and offers guest activities that included "boating, fishing, and a good day's tramp over mountain trails to Estes Park." *Courtesy of Jane Kemp*.

Nell Donathan married into the Young family in 1921 when she became the bride of Josie's son Jake. The Youngs would spend their first years together helping Josie at the Rustic Hotel. Eventually they owned their own business called the Mountain Home Café and Cabins located on Vine Street. After the death of her husband Jake in 1949, Nell married Paul Pauly. In 1961, Nell became an author when she wrote *Ghosts of the Shootin'*. Nell and Pauly sold the business and retired in the 1970s. $15+.

Columbine Lake is located one mile northwest of Grand Lake. At first the enterprise consisted of the small lake and approximately ten rustic cabins. By the 1950s some updating had occurred with "modern cabins" being advertised by owners Mr. and Mrs. Howard Breckon. Under the ownership of Jim Isenhart in the late 1960s, the property was subdivided into residential lots. A Columbine Lake cabin is shown in this F. P. Clatworthy hand-colored postcard. Circa 1920s, $20+.

This view, labeled "Cross Rd. Service Sta., Grand Lake, Colo.," dates from the 1930s. The business was also called Cross Roads Cottage Camp. It was owned by Mr. and Mrs. Harvey Hatton and was located near the old road in Grand Lake that turned off from U.S. Highway 34. The business was later purchased by Jim Robinson, who renamed it the El Navajo Lodge. $20+.

The Kauffman House is the only one of the early Grand Lake hotels still standing. It was built by Ezra Kauffman and was placed on the National Register of Historic Places in 1974. Ezra was a silver miner in Lulu City, sixteen miles north of Grand Lake during its heyday, which lasted from 1879-1883. Other mining towns had also sprung up in the area and Grand Lake bustled with activity as prospectors purchased supplies for their mining endeavors. After the mining boom ended, Grand Lake was left in decline as settlers abandoned the area. When Kauffman left Lulu City, he married and settled in nearby Hot Sulphur Springs. In 1892 the couple and their two children moved to Grand Lake where they began building their hotel, which grew with added additions through the years. Because of the hard life they were living, Kauffman's wife soon left the area taking their children with her. Erza Kauffman remarried in 1907, and with his second wife, Belle, three daughters were born. He died in 1920 and the family continued to run the business as a summer hotel until 1946. It was purchased by the Grand Lake Area Historical Society in 1973 and is now operating as a museum. *Courtesy of Grand Lake Area Historical Society.*

Rapids Hotel was built by John Lapsley Ish and opened in 1915. It is located on the Tonatutu River, commonly called the North Inlet. Ish built the hotel using lodgepole pines from the area, which were cut from his own sawmill. He also provided running water and electricity to the hotel using a water wheel he constructed in the nearby river. Sanborn postcard, circa early 1940s, $20+.

The bar and lounge at the Rapids Hotel. Ish sold the lodge in the early 1940s and moved to Boulder, Colorado, along with wife Alice before he died in 1943. The lodge has had a number of owners since then and past rumors of gambling, prostitution, and bootleg liquor add to its colorful history. Sanborn postcard, circa 1940s, $20+.

This Sanborn postcard shows the lounge at the Rapids furnished with bamboo-type furniture. Besides the hotel, Ish constructed rental cabins on the property. In 1934 prices at the hotel were $5 to $6 per day per person or $30 to $37.50 a week. The hotel then had a capacity for one hundred guests. Circa 1940s, $20+.

The Pine Cone Inn was also an Ish family project. In 1923 the *Estes Park Trail* announced Leslie Ish, John's son, was building a Pine Cone Cabaret that summer. Leslie was the operator of the Pine Cone Inn for many years. The original Pine Cone building was rectangular in shape and had been constructed on the site of the old Grand Lake House, an early hotel built in 1878. Sanborn postcard, $20+.

PINE CONE INN
Grand Lake Colorado

DANCE

To the Music of

VIC SCHILLING
AND HIS ORCHESTRA

CHICKEN, STEAK AND TROUT DINNERS

Telephone 10

BALL ROOM - PINE CONE INN - GRAND LAKE, COLO.

The Pine Cone Inn was popular for its dances as well as its amateur night contests. Shown is a Sanborn postcard of the ballroom along with a card advertising dances, music, and food. For many years, tickets cost only ten cents a dance. In a 1941 advertisement, Mrs. Leslie (Goldie) Ish was listed as the owner since her husband had been killed earlier in a car accident. Postcard, $20+; dance ticket, $15.

The Pine Cone Inn was destroyed by fire on October 5, 1943. The rebuilt inn featured a circular structure called the Wagon Wheel Bar as shown in this Sanborn postcard. A menu from the era lists trout, soup, salad, vegetable, and dessert all for $1. Mrs. Goldie Ish and her children were the owners. Postcard, $20+; menu, $15+.

PINE CONE INN
Grand Lake Colorado

WAGON WHEEL BAR AND COCKTAIL LOUNGE - PINE CONE INN - GRAND LAKE

Mrs. Goldie Ish and Children

The well-known Corner Cupboard located at the intersection of Grand Avenue and Pitkin Street had its beginning as the Grand Central Hotel and Restaurant built in 1880. It was owned and operated by Winslow Nickerson and his wife Lillian. Part of Grand Central housed the first school in 1881-82. Mr. and Mrs. Henry W. Rhone purchased it in 1919 and it became the Corner Cupboard Tea Room in 1920. It eventually included a hotel and dining room with food recommended by Duncan Hines. $20+.

By the 1940s the Corner Cupboard Restaurant and Hotel had a capacity for 150 guests and included twenty lakeside cottages for rent. Promotional materials were sent by the Rhones to encourage prospective guests to "spend your vacation where there is a combination of mountains and water." Postcard, $10+; pamphlet, $10.

In addition to the Corner Cupboard property, the Rhones owned the Wiswall Tavern and Hotel located on Grand Avenue. It was built in 1910 and has since been operated as a lodge, tavern, private dwelling, art gallery, and restaurant. Sanborn postcard, circa early 1930s, $20+.

DINING ROOM · CORNER CUPBOARD · GRAND LAKE, COLO.

Sanborn postcard of Corner Cupboard Dining Room when dinners were priced as low as eighty-five cents. Pies cost fifteen cents and banana splits were twenty-five cents. Circa 1950s, $10+.

The Rhones offered a number of historic cabins for rent as part of their holdings including the Pioneer Cabin, which was the town's first framed building; the Podunk Cottage, which had once served as the county clerk's office; and Skybrand Cottage, which had served not only as a schoolhouse but the teacher's home as well. Shown are the Corner Cupboard rental cottages with prime lake views. Sanborn postcard, $15+.

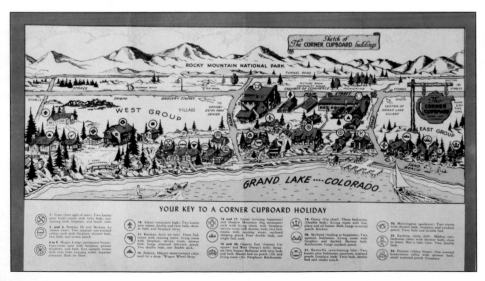

This brochure shows a map of the various cabins and hotels that were available for rent by the Corner Cupboard. The cabins then numbered thirty. The Corner Cupboard itself included the office and dining room, while the historic Kauffman House was being used for a gift shop and rental bedrooms. Henry Rhone died in 1955. By 1958 new owners Mr. and Mrs. M. D. Whaley were operating the restaurant and hotel, while Carolyn Rhone was still renting many cottages in the area. Mrs. Rhone died in 1965. The Corner Cupboard Restaurant continued as an important fixture in the community until it was torn down in 1999. Circa 1950, $20+.

Daven Haven Lodge was built in the 1930s and was owned and operated by Lester and Cornelia Piper and Mrs. Piper's mother, Mrs. Lela C. Davis. By the mid-1960s Daven Haven was being featured in several Gray Line bus tour packages that included lodging and meals. Gray Line lodging options also included the Stanley Hotel in Estes Park. Postcard by American Graphics, of Denver, Colorado, circa 1960s, $10-12.

Guests took their meals in the knotty pine dining room at Daven Haven Lodge in the Pines, where logs crackled in the big fireplace every morning and evening. Postcard by Artvue Post Card Co., of New York, New York, $15+.

CORNER OF DINING ROOM AT DAVEN HAVEN CAMP
GRAND LAKE, COLORADO

The Daven Haven enterprise eventually included the nearby Lake Lodge that was built as a private residence by Jim Furlong in the late 1920s to early 1930s. After World War II, the lake home was purchased by the Pipers and Mrs. Davis and was added to the Daven Haven operation. The Lake Lodge contains 6,000 square feet of space including eleven bedrooms. Guests at both lodges enjoyed the private beach, boats, and water skiing. A card room, pool room, and planned entertainment were also provided for the guests. Sanborn 1950s postcard, $10+; brochure, $15.

Grand Lake, Colorado

The DAVEN HAVEN Lodges

Shown is the Daven Haven Lake Lodge lobby, furnished with the wicker furniture from earlier years. The original fireplace was still in use. Postcard by Dexter, of West Nyack, New York. Circa 1960s, $15+.

This view shows the beach, boats, and guests staying at the Daven Haven Lake Lodge, which was sold by Tom and Betty Sowell in 1983 to a four-way partnership that included the Bells, Larsons, Zicks, and Beachs. The Daven Haven Lake Lodge is now called the Lake Haven. The Lodge in the Pines, located across the road, was sold by the Pipers to Tom and Betty Sowell in 1968 and is now owned by Greg and Carey Barnes. Postcard by Dexter Press, Inc. Circa 1960s, $6-8.

THE KAROSE

The KaRose Resort came about as the result of a planned railroad line that was to run from Granby to Monarch Lake and on to Grand Lake. In addition, the Rocky Mountain Railway Co. built a small company town also called Monarch circa 1905. The track from the Granby area to Monarch was completed in 1907, according to Robert C. Black III, author of *Island in the Rockies*. Although the railroad never succeeded, many of the town structures were eventually used in a summer resort called KaRose, named after Katherine Rose Dierks, a daughter of the owner. Advertisements offered hiking, boating, fishing, hunting, tennis, croquet, archery, bowling, billiards, golfing, horseback riding, cards, and dancing. The resort was popular with families and many groups returned each summer. Postcard by Rocky Mountain View Co., of Denver, Colorado. Circa 1930s, $20+.

"KaRose, Colorado, 'Where the World Stays Young,' Granby, Colorado." Townspeople from the Grand Lake and Granby areas also took advantage of the resort's close proximity with bowling and Sunday dinners a favorite combination. Unlike many of the early hotels and resorts, which were destroyed by fire, KaRose ended its life as the result of water. It unfortunately lay in the path of what would become the new Granby Lake reservoir and the buildings that could be saved were moved to new locations while others were dismantled or destroyed. The three-lane bowling alley was moved to Granby where it was put to good use by the townspeople for many years. $30+.

KAROSE

The Lake

Grand Lake has been the center for activities in Grand Lake Village since its beginning. It is the reason for the town's existence and the growing number of vacation homes that now exist throughout the area. The lake will forever serve to attract visitors who marvel at its natural setting as they enjoy the many recreational opportunities created by its wonderful presence.

FRANK S. THAYER, PUBLISHER, DENVER.

NO. 725.—MT. CRAIG, GRAND LAKE, COLO.

Hand-colored view of Grand Lake. The message on the back reads, "Spent night here on stage drive around the Park which takes about two days." The writer was a guest of Roe Emery's Circle Tour. F. P. Clatworthy postcard. Circa 1920s, $20+.

Early view of Grand Lake with Mt. Craig, also known as Mt. Baldy, elevation 12,005 feet, in the background. Postcard by Frank S. Thayer, of Denver, Colorado, was postmarked June 25, 1909. $12-15.

Even though transportation was difficult in the early days of Grand Lake, summer visitors arrived by stage coach beginning in the late 1880s for vacations spent in the early hotels. It wasn't long until summer homes were being constructed around the lake. Many of the building materials had to be brought to the home sites by boat because no roads were available. A few of these cabins continue to have limited access even today. This view, labeled "Towing House Logs, Grand Lake, Colo.," shows a boat with the logs being pulled along behind in the lake waters. $20+.

Unlike most of the cabins built around Grand Lake, this one was constructed on the top of a rock formation. It was owned by the J. R. Ives family for many years. Mr. Ives was Commodore of the Grand Lake Yacht Club in 1923. The cabin can still be seen on its high perch on the lake's north side. Out West Photo Shop, of Boulder, Colorado. $15+.

Photo postcard of the lake home of the Earl Coryell family. Mr. Coryell was Commodore of the Grand Lake Yacht Club from 1948-1950. Many of the lake homes have been owned by the same families for generations. Circa 1940, $10+.

THE EARL CORYELL'S   GRAND LAKE, COLO.

This view shows a lake house duplex that was built on adjoining lots in 1909 by the Batty and Keester families of Alma, Nebraska, for use as a summer retreat. It is located on Grand Lake's south shore. The Batty family has since acquired the adjoining duplex, known as "Anna's Cabin," which is available for short-term rental during the summer. $15+.

Several famous people have been attracted to Grand Lake's allure and have purchased lakeside property to use as summer homes. One of the most well-known was Joyce Hall, founder of Hallmark Cards, whose family members still use the home. John Thompson, the originator of the red piano books titled *John Thompson's Modern Course for the Piano*, also owned a summer home. Shown is the sheet music for one of his compositions called "Shadows on Grand Lake" published in 1939 by The Willis Music Co. His home on the west shore of the lake also remains in use by his family. Another prominent summer resident was William H. Hoffstot, who bought a lake cabin in 1911 and named it Sunshine. He invented and patented the Sunshine lantern, which was later purchased by the Coleman Company of Wichita, Kansas. $20+.

The Grand Lake Yacht Club was incorporated in 1902 by Richard Crawford Campbell, William Harry Bryant, and J. Fermor Spencer. The clubhouse was built in 1912 on land donated by Jacob N. Pettingell. Known as the highest yacht club anchorage in the world, it was honored in 1912 when Irish yachtsman Sir Thomas J. Lipton presented a silver trophy cup to be awarded by the club. Albertype Co. postcard, $20+.

This view is labeled, "Watching Boat Races, Grand Lake, Colo., Out West Photo, Boulder." The Grand Lake Yacht Club can be seen in the background. Circa 1915, $20+.

The first sailboat was introduced on the lake by William Harry Bryant in 1903, replacing make-shift vessels that had been fashioned from rowboats and bed sheets. The first official sailboat races were held in August 1903 when the Colorado Cup was won by Bryant in his new sailboat Dorothy II. Hand-colored postcard of the Grand Lake Yacht Club published by F. P. Clatworthy, circa late 1920s, $25+.

YACHT RACES DURING REGATTA WEEK, AT GRAND LAKE, COLO

This Sepia view is labeled "Yacht Races during Regatta Week at Grand Lake, Colo." A similar Sepia photograph decorates the pictured bridge tally issued by F. J. Francis of Estes Park. Postcard, $8-10; bridge tally, $20.

N126:—GRAND LAKE, COLORADO

Sailboat races were suspended during the World War II years. This view of the Grand Lake Yacht Club was postmarked in 1942 and was used by a soldier as he traveled on a troop train close to his hometown in Mansfield, Ohio. He writes, "Hi Sugar. I think I may go thru Mansfield tonite so I am writing this now to toss out a window. Hope someone finds it. We are going thru Indiana now. Wish I could jump off and come and see you. Lots of love, Woody." At the bottom of the card, he has written, "Finder, please mail this." Evidently someone followed the soldier's instructions and mailed the card as intended. Denver News Co. postcard, $8-10.

This Sanborn view shows a yacht race on Grand Lake. Also pictured is the *Denver and Colorado Hotel Greeters Guide* dated August 15-22, 1941. "Regatta Week" is featured on the front cover. It is held in August each year. Circa 1937, postcard, $8-10; magazine, $12.

Shown is an early water skier at Grand Lake. Postcard marked "Water Sports at Grand Lake, Colo. Out West Photo Boulder." Circa late 1920s, $20+.

A water skier from later years ends his chilly adventure at the public dock with the beach in the background. Sanborn postcard, $3-5.

This aerial view shows the beach, shore line, the Yacht Club, and the boat docks. On the right of this postcard are several of the cabins rented by Corner Cupboard for many years. Although these cabins are no longer there, the Yacht Club and the public marina remain as familiar landmarks. On warm summer days, boat rentals thrive as visitors take a ride before they experience their next 'circle tour' adventure. This could include a trip over Trail Ridge Road, a hike to Adams Falls, or a stroll along the boardwalk on Grand Avenue. Flatiron Post Card Co., circa 1960s, $6-8.

Bibliography

Books

Bancroft, Caroline. *Grand Lake from Utes to Yachts: A Legendary History*. Boulder, Colorado: Johnson Publishing Co., 1982.

Bancroft, Caroline. *Trail Ridge Country: The Romantic History of Estes Park and Grand Lake*. Boulder, Colorado: Johnson Publishing Co., 1968.

Black, Robert C. III. *Island in the Rockies: the Pioneer Era of Grand County, Colorado*. Granby, Colorado: Grand County Pioneer Society, 1969.

Cairns, Mary Lyons. *Grand Lake in the Olden Days: A compilation of Grand Lake, the Pioneers and the Olden Days*. Denver, Colorado: The World Press, Inc., 1971.

Clinger, Mic, James H. Pickering, and Carey Stevanus. *Estes Park and Rocky Mountain National Park: Then & Now*. Westcliffe, Colorado: Westcliffe Publishers, 2006.

Geary, Michael H. *A Quick History of Grand Lake Including Rocky Mountain National Park and the Grand Lake Lodge*. Ouray, Colorado: Western Reflections, 1999.

Gray, Avis, Ann Feucht, and Ryan Gray. *Voices of Courage from a Rocky Mountain Village in Their Own Spirit*. Grand Lake, Colorado: Self-published, 2002.

Lindberg, James, Patricia Raney, and Janet Robertson. John Gunn, Editor. *Rocky Mountain Rustic: Historic Buildings of the Rocky Mountain National Park Area*. Estes Park, Colorado: Rocky Mountain Nature Association, 2004.

Melton, Jack R. and Lulabeth Melton. *YMCA of the Rockies: Reflections, Traditions & Vision*. Estes Park, Colorado: YMCA of the Rockies, 2006.

Mills, Enos A. *The Story of Early Estes Park, Rocky Mountain National Park and Grand Lake*. Estes Park, Colorado: Robert H. and Enda M. Kiley, 1986.

O'Ryan, Dorothy O'Donnell. *Sailing Above the Clouds*. Montrose, Colorado: Western Reflections Publishing Company, 2002.

Pauly, Nell. *Ghosts of the Shootin'*. Grand Lake, Colorado: Kaufman Press, 1961.

Pedersen, Henry F. *Those Castles of Wood: the Story of Early Lodges of Rocky Mountain National Park and Pioneer Days of Estes Park, Colorado*. Estes Park, Colorado: Self-published, 1993.

Smith, Lois. *The Baldpate Collections Millennium Edition*. Baldpate Inn, Estes Park, Colorado: Baldpate Inn, 2000.

Brochures and Pamphlets

Colorado Rocky Mountain National (Estes) Park, Burlington Route. Chicago, Illinois: Poole Bros., Inc., 1930.

Directory and Official Tourist Information: Rocky Mountain Region. Denver, Colorado: Highway Publishing Company, 1924.

Enos Mills Cabin Museum & Gallery. Estes Park, Colorado. Promotional Brochure, 2006.

Indian Springs Resort. Information and history promotional pamphlet, Idaho Springs, Colorado: 2006.

The Kauffman House. Grand Lake, Colorado: Grand Lake Area Historical Society, 1997.

Kaye, Glen. *Guide to Holzwarth Trout Lodge Historic Site*. Estes Park, Colorado: Rocky Mountain Nature Association, 2003.

Rapids Lodge. "Our History." Printed history supplied by Rapids Lodge and obituary from *Middle Park Times*, January 14, 1943.

River Forks Inn Historic Stage Stop. Menu and "100 Year History" supplied by River Forks Inn. Drake, Colorado, 2006.

Rocky Mountain Motor Company. Denver, Colorado. Promotional brochures for the Circle Tour and other Rocky Mountain National Park attractions, circa 1922, 1928, 1932, 1941, 1951, and 1959.

Rocky Mountain National Park, Colorado. United States Department of the Interior, National Park Service. Washington, D.C.: Government Printing Office, 1934.

Rocky Mountain National Park, Colorado, United States Railroad Administration. *National Park Series*. Chicago, Illinois: Press of Faulkner-Ryan Co., 1919.

Rocky Mountain National Park, Estes Park, Colorado, Burlington Route. Chicago, Illinois: Poole Bros., 1926.

Rocky Mountain National Park Estes Park, Colorado. Omaha, Nebraska: Union Pacific, early 1920s.

Visitors' Tour Brochure. Stanley Hotel. Estes Park, Colorado, 2006.

A Walking Tour of Historic Grand Lake. Grand Lake, Colorado: Grand Lake Historical Society, undated.

Magazines, Newspapers & Newsletters

"A Week in Estes Park, Colorado." *The Hotel Monthly*. July 1910, pp. 35-41.

Asbury, Tim. "Salvation Army purchases historic Longs Peak Inn site." *Estes Park Trail-Gazette*. Estes Park, Colorado: November 6, 1991.

Boyer, Barb. "The Lost Lodges of Rocky Mountain National Park." *Estes Park Trail-Gazette*. Estes Park, Colorado: July 2, 2002.

Bradley, Bob. "Historic Hidden Valley." Estes Park, Colorado: Historic Hidden Valley Association, November 3, 1993.

Buchholtz, C. W. "Paradise Founded." *Colorado Heritage*. Denver, Colorado: Colorado Historical Society, 1984.

Busch, Mel. "How the Village Became a Town: This Week in History." *Estes Park Trail-Gazette*. Estes Park, Colorado: April 20, 1983.

Cone, Wyane. "Park Celebrating 60th Anniversary, Bill Became Law on Jan. 26th, 1915." *Estes Park Trail-Gazette*. Estes Park, Colorado: January 24, 1975.

"Enos A. Mills, Author, Nature Guide and Pioneer of Estes Park Departs From This Life." *Estes Park Trail*. Estes Park, Colorado: September 22, 1922.

"Estes Fish Hatchery Lures area Visitors." *Estes Park Trail*. Estes Park, Colorado: August 15, 1969.

"Fire Strikes a Double Blow at Riverside Hotel." *Estes Park Trail*. Estes Park, Colorado: December 14, 1956.

"Facts on Hidden Valley." *Estes Park Trail-Gazette*. Estes Park, Colorado: 1974.

Grand Lake Pioneer. Various advertisements. Grand Lake, Colorado: July 20, 1940.

Jessen, Ken. "Glen Haven Cabins were once Religious Retreats." *Loveland Reporter-Herald*. Loveland, Colorado: June 29, 2003.

Jessen, Ken. "Longs Peak Inn was Founded by Guides." *Loveland Reporter-Herald*. Loveland, Colorado: June 6, 2004.

Johnson, Keith. "Trail Ridge Store is the place to shop at the top." *Daily Reporter-Herald*. Loveland, Colorado: October 17, 1990.

Lloyd, James V. "Supt. Lloyd Welcomes You to This Great Playground of the Rockies." *Sky-Hi News Vacation Edition*. Granby, Colorado: April 25, 1958.

Web Sites

"Runoff blamed in ditch collapse." *Longmont Times*. Longmont, Colorado. June 8, 2003.

Marranzino, Pasquale. "Father of Colorado Tourism Hale at 75." *Rocky Mountain News*. Denver, Colorado: October 30, 1949.

McHendrie, Frances. "A personal reminiscence of life on Phantom Valley Ranch." *Grand Lake: The First 100 Years, An Alpenglow Magazine Centennial Supplement*. Winter Park, Colorado: 1981.

Metzler, Brian. "Longs-distance calling. Rewards plentiful for conquering one of state's top peaks." *Rocky Mountain News*. Denver, Colorado: July 1, 2006.

"Manford House Opened for Business." *Mountaineer*. Estes Park, Colorado: June 11, 1908.

Munnings, Bill. *The Colorado Hotel Greeters Guide*. August 17-23, 1941.

Rahn, Laurie. "Homespun Haven." *Estes Park Trail Gazette*. Estes Park, Colorado: July 22, 1994.

"Summer Theatre Comes to Grand Lake and Area." *Sky-Hi News Vacation Edition*. Granby, Colorado: May, 1967.

"The Little Church in the Pines" and "New St. Anne's Church in Grand Lake." *Sky-Hi News Vacation Edition*. Granby, Colorado: April 25, 1958.

Tardani, Philip. "Park cemetery is just Grand." *Loveland Reporter-Herald*. Loveland, Colorado: September 21-22, 1996.

Whaley, Monte. "Hidden Valley reborn for year 'round fun." *Denver Post*. Denver, Colorado: December 1, 2004.

Whaley, Monte. "Town fights for its name. Larimer County plan would strip Glen Haven from addresses." *Denver Post*. Denver, Colorado: October 30, 2006.

Widmer, Ann. "Grand Lake: Little town is proud of its rustic style." *Daily Reporter-Herald*. Loveland, Colorado: October 17, 1990.

Widmer, Ann. "The Other Side, Park shows another face across Continental Divide." *Daily Reporter-Herald*. Loveland, Colorado: October 17, 1990.

Batty lake house duplex guest rental, Grand Lake, Colorado. www.annas-place.com.

Baldpate Inn, www.baldpateinn.com.

Daven Haven Lodge, www.davenhavenlodge.com.

Estes Park Aerial Tramway, www.estestram.com.

Grand Lake Lodge. "History of the Grand Lake Lodge and Surrounding Area." www.grandlakelodge.com.

Marys Lake Lodge, www.maryslakelodge.com.

National Register of Historic Places, www.nationalregister-ofhistoricplaces.com.

Park Theatre, www.parktheatre.com.

Rooftop Rodeo, www.rooftoprodeo.com.

Town of Estes Park Web site. "The Lawn Lake Flood." www.estesnet.com.

Wild Basin Lodge & Event Center, Allenspark, Colorado. www.wildbasinlodge.com.

Index